The Book of Ogham

ABOUT THE AUTHOR

Edred Thorsson is well known as the author of such books as *Futhark: A Handbook of Rune Magic, Runelore: A Handbook of Esoteric Runology, At the Well of Wyrd: A Handbook of Runic Divination, Rune-Might* and *A Book of Troth*. Since 1972, he has been dedicated to the esoteric and exoteric study of the Indo-European, Celtic and Teutonic traditions. He studied Old Irish, Middle Welsh and Indo-European religion and culture at major universities in Germany and in the United States. *The Book of Ogham* represents a practical magical synthesis of his work in the Celtic field.

TO WRITE TO THE AUTHOR

If you wish to contact the author or would like more information about this book, please write to the author in care of Llewellyn Worldwide and we will forward your request. Both the author and publisher appreciate hearing from you and learning of your enjoyment of this book and how it has helped you. Llewellyn Worldwide cannot guarantee that every letter written to the author can be answered, but all will be forwarded. Please write to:

Edred Thorsson
c/o Llewellyn Worldwide
P.O. Box 64383-783, St. Paul, MN 55164-0383, U.S.A.

Please enclose a self-addressed, stamped envelope for reply, or $1.00 to cover costs.
If outside U.S.A., enclose international postal reply coupon.

FREE CATALOG FROM LLEWELLYN

For more than 90 years Llewellyn has brought its readers knowledge in the fields of metaphysics and human potential. Learn about the newest books in spiritual guidance, natural healing, astrology, occult philosophy and more. Enjoy book reviews, new age articles, a calendar of events, plus current advertised products and services. To get your free copy of the *Llewellyn's New Worlds of Mind and Spirit*, send your name and address to:

Llewellyn's New Worlds of Mind and Spirit
P.O. Box 64383-783, St. Paul, MN 55164-0383, U.S.A.

THE CELTIC TREE ORACLE

EDRED THORSSON

Illustrated by Anne Marie Hoppe

1994
Llewellyn Publications, St. Paul, MN 55164-0383

FIRST EDITION
Second Printing, 1994

Cover and illustrations by Anne Marie Hoppe
Layout by Terry Buske

Library of Congress Cataloging-in-Publication Data
Thorsson, Edred
    The book of ogham : the Celtic tree oracle / Edred Thorsson
        p. cm.
    ISBN 0-87542-783-9
    1. Includes bibliographical references. 2. Magic, Celtic. 3. Runes—Miscellanea..
4. Trees—Miscellanea. I. Title. II. Title Celtic tree oracle.
BF1622.C45T56   1992 IN PROCESS
133.3'089'916—dc20   92-13330
                                                                                 CIP

Llewellyn Publications
A Division of Llewellyn Worldwide, Ltd.
P.O. 64383, St. Paul, MN 55164-0383

To My Celtic Ancestors
and for Crystal Dawn

Also by Edred Thorsson

Futhark: A Handbook of Rune Magic
  (Samuel Weiser, Inc., 1984)

Runelore: A Handbook of Esoteric Runology (Weiser, 1987)

At the Well of Wyrd:
  A Handbook of Runic Divination (Weiser, 1988)

The Truth About Teutonic Magick (Llewellyn, 1989)

A Book of Troth (Llewellyn, 1989)

Rune Might (Llewellyn, 1989)

The Nine Doors of Midgard (Llewellyn, 1991)

Northern Magic (Llewellyn, 1992)

As S. Edred Flowers

Fire and Ice (Llewellyn, 1990)

Acknowledgments

I would like to thank my academic mentors, whose sense of objective sympathy I would like to think makes itself felt in this work. In addition, I would like to acknowledge the help and encouragement provided by Michael Rigby, James Allen Chisholm, and most of all Tadhg MacCrossan, Ard-Drui of Druidiactos, for his careful reading and correction of the manuscript.

Abbreviations

BCE   Before the Common Era (= BC)

CE   Common Era (= AD)

O. Ir. Old Irish

A Note on the Pronunciation of Foreign Words—
In the text, Old Irish words are often followed by a guide to their phonetic pronunciation. These are included in square brackets.

Table of Contents

Introduction

For centuries now, people of Celtic descent, and even those who have deep and abiding sympathies for the Celtic ways, have been trying to revivify the largely lost lore of ancient Celtic spirituality. Much of the effort at revival has been aimed in the direction of the Druids, the elder (pre-Christian) priesthood of the Celts. For the most part, this has been a failed experiment, as the would-be revivalists almost invariably used non-Celtic keys to try to unlock the mysteries of the Celts. This manual is one attempt to recover the methods and systems of Celtic thought to help in the task of unlocking not only the outer mysteries of the ancient Celtic Druids, but also at the same time reveal a way to find paths to inner truths about the self of the bard and how that self relates to the world outside itself.

This kind of book has long been needed. Its historical and cosmological lore is based on the best available thought on the subjects—not rooted in the fantasies and forgeries that have unfortunately all too often beset the effort to restore the Celtic tradition. At the same time it is a *practical* manual. It is part of a system which must be studied and experienced through actual *work* with the oghamic tradition and the fews of the ogham oracle. Other treatments of ogham, such as Robert Graves' *The White Goddess* or, more recently, Colin Murray's *The Celtic Tree Oracle,* have represented attempts to breathe life into the Celtic tradition, but they have been flawed by their acceptance or invention of "poetic truths" to replace or displace reliable historical and traditional truths, which are the true pathways to the inner knowledge and wisdom of the ancient and eternal Celts. Graves is useful as a collection of lore about the individual fews, or "trees," but the system and history he proposes for it is nontraditional.

The inner purpose of *this* work is the awakening of the deeply rooted structural patterns of the Celtic psyche or soul in the very being of the bard. This book can only be a small part of such an all-encompassing and enormous task. The reader would be greatly aided in this through the study of such fine works as *Elements of the Celtic Tradition* by Caitlin Matthews, *Celtic Heritage* by the Brothers Rees and most especially by the practical approach of *The Sacred Cauldron* by Tadhg MacCrossan. This is a work of spiritual awakening and reawakening.

The Book of Ogham presents a complete system of *divination* much like that one might encounter with the runes or the tarot. Beyond this outer purpose of teaching an oracular system, however, the work helps to open up a mysterious or hidden world from within the bard—it helps the bard to *find* the objective inner truth of various matters concealed deep within the self. It seeks to do this according to a traditional system so that, beyond learning only of the individual self, the bard becomes knowledgeable and ultimately *wise* within a tradition that transcends that individual self. In doing this, the bard becomes part of the eternal stream of tradition and begins to drink directly from the true cauldron of inspiration.

It must be remembered that *The Book of Ogham* is *not* a complete system of Celtic lore, initiation or magick. It is only a part of the puzzle, or a piece of a vast knotwork of being and tradition yet waiting to be loosened and understood by those who will re-establish the traditions of true Celtic spirituality.

In the course of this work, the bard will be presented with the actual history of the Celtic oghams, and the question of the relationship of the runic system to that of ogham will be discussed in detail. Most important to any true and deep understanding of a divinatory system is a grasp of the cosmology and theoretical context of the system. We will therefore spend some time exploring the pertinent lore of the wondrous Celtic cosmology—or lore concerning the structure of the universe. It is in this context that all events occurred, occur and will occur. Therefore, cosmology is the context in which the ogham fews are cast and the truth revealed. The latter part of the book gives full and detailed instructions on how to actually carry out divinatory workings with the ogham fews and how to interpret the ogham figures in actual readings.

The secret lore and practices of the ancient Celtic Druids have long been the object of speculation and exploration by those who would call themselves modern-day Druids. Although I would not call myself that, I have come into possession of certain methodological secrets shared by the Druids and Drightens of old. I spent many years studying ancient Celtic lore, including the languages of Old Irish and Middle Welsh—the languages in which most of the old Celtic lore is to be found. Of course, most of my work has been done with Teutonic runes—with which I am most at home.

The Book of Ogham is a purely *Celtic* system. In exploring and working the system, the bard will come to understand the Celtic way to new depths and will come to know the inner workings of the self and its relationship to and interactions with the world outside in a timeless way. The true and inner *learning* of oghams is a pathway to inner knowledge and can, for some, become the systematic way to gain the kind of understanding necessary to attainment of the level of knowledge traditionally known by such poetic names as the salmon or tooth of knowledge. Read, study and work to learn how to drink deeply from the very source of the traditional lore of the Druids.

—Edred Thorsson
Austin, Texas
Samhain 1989 e.v.

Oghamic Knowledge

Chapter 1

The Roots of the Knowledge of Trees

Ogham is just one of the many ways the ancient Celts encoded their secret wisdom. Of those ways, it is one of the few that we can still gain access to today. We can do this because enough clues were left behind from the genuine and authentic lore of the past to allow us to reconstruct the system from within the body of actual Celtic thought.

The ogham system is deeply rooted in the Celtic world view. Just as the Germanic runes were never used by Celts, ogham was never used by any other people. As such, it represents a unique and particular expression of wisdom within a certain set of symbols and myths. One might try to use ogham-wisdom to unlock the secrets of Greek mythology, but it would certainly prove to be a highly frustrating exercise, not to mention a deceptive one.

So, who are/were the Celts?

The Celts were an identifiable ethnic (national) and linguistic group of people who differentiated themselves from their Indo-European cultural matrix as early as 2000 BCE. The various Indo-European groups began to migrate out of the region of the Caspian Sea as early as 4000 BCE, with various

individual linguistic and national groups differentiating themselves out of that larger primeval group at various times after that. The original homeland of the Celts—that is, where a group of pre-Celtic tribes came into being as true Celts—seems to have been central Europe (approximately present-day Switzerland, Austria, and southern Germany).

Although we now very much identify the British Isles as having originally been Celtic, these lands were not actually "Celticized" (by invasions of Celts from the continent) until as late as 700 to 500 BCE.

From some early time there was a linguistic (and perhaps cultural) split within the Celtic world. This is exemplified in the language by a dialect split between the so-called P-Celts and the Q-Celts. The P-Celts are the Brythonic peoples of Britain and Gaul, and the Q-Celts are the Goidelic tribes of Ireland—who also later colonized present-day Scotland. Examples of the differences in the languages can be shown through a look at the basic words for "four" and "five" in the two language groups:

	Old Irish	**Middle Welsh**
four:	*cethir* [kyethir]	*pedwar* [ped-war]
five:	*coic* [koyg]	*pump* [pimp]

These linguistic differences must have signified and led to a number of cultural differences as well. This is one of the reasons why we concentrate on the Irish tradition in this book—Ireland the source of the bulk of the oldest mythological material and it is where ogham was most strongly represented.

For those who for whatever reason wish to resist the idea that the Celtic mythology and religion (as well as culture) is essentially based on Indo-European roots, it might be noted that the first element in the names *Ire*-land and *Ira*-n are the same linguistically, and both are related to the *Arya*-ns of India.

Thus the great span of Indo-European culture, from the middle of Asia to the westernmost islands of Europe, can be seen in its full expanse from ancient times.

The Oghamic System

Ogham is not like other writing systems, magical or profane, which you might have encountered. It is really an alphabetic code more than an alphabet as such. It is a system of numerical codes or signs which stand for sounds or letters. The sound system is as follows:

B	L	F	S	N
H	D	T	C	Q
M	G	NG	Z	R
A	O	U	E	I

From this arrangement, it can be seen that there are four groups (O.Ir. *aicme*) of five letters each in the system. From this, codes making use of these letters or sounds in this arrangement can be made. For example, the formula 1:4 would mean: first group, fourth letter = S. In classic ogham epigraphy (inscriptions) the system shown in figure 1.1 is used.

At a later time there were five additional signs added to the ogham system to represent diphthongs. That these are later additions and not part of the original system is shown both by the Irish name for them (*forfedha*), which means "additional

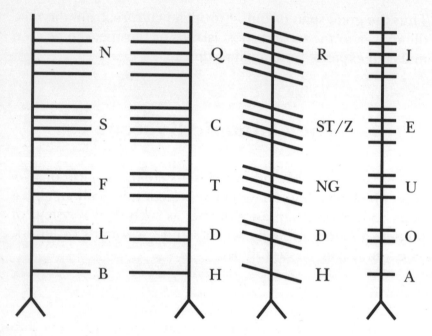

Figure 1.1: The Original Ogham System

tree or letter," and by the fact that these signs are not used in the pre-medieval inscriptions. However, it is important to note that the *forfedha* are cosmographic signs of traditional value; it is just that their esoteric function is substantially different from those of the basic 20 oghamic *fedha*, or "fews," as they are called in Anglicized form.

It should be noted that the names of the *forfedha* are not as essential as those of the other fews. They were certainly added at a later time. There is substantial disagreement among scholars as to the forms and names of these fews, but here we have symbolic shapes to guide us in our determination of their cosmological and divinatory meanings. The *forfedha* clearly stand outside the normal numerical sequence of the 20 fews of the basic system.

Table 1.1: The Historical Forms of the Forfedha

Shape	Sound	Name	Meaning of Name
	ae	*phagos*	beech
	io	*iphin*	gooseberry
	ui	*uileand*	honeysuckle
	oi	*oir*	spindle
	ea	*ebad*	aspen (alternate name of E-few)

What is essential to realize about the secret of the oghamic tradition is that it is a numerical code based on a set of sounds. The bardic system of classification is based on the fact that things belonging to one secret class or another all start with the same sound. On another level, those things which have names that start with the same sound will alliterate in bardic poetic composition—and thus further reveal the hidden and poetic connections between the words.

The oghamic system consists of three components:

1. Sound

2. Number(s) [order and twofold indication of its place in the system]

3. Name(s)

The sound and the name are linked by the acrophonic or "first-sound" principle, while the numerical code both reveals the sound and conceals it behind a veil of esoteric knowledge. All of these aspects have a certain importance of their own.

The structure of the ogham system is determined by two

factors: (1) shape (i.e., the kind of shape a sign has)—which determines the *aicme* of the sign—and (2) number (i.e., how many of these kinds of shapes there are), which determines the position of the character inside the *aicme*.

Many variant forms of ogham based on these principles of construction are found in the text of *The Book of Ballymote*. These are based on a technique very similar to that used in the construction of runic codes among the Germanic peoples (see chapter 2). For example, the distinct consonants of "shield ogham" (O.Ir. *ogam airenach*) appear:

At some time, probably very early, the letters were most commonly designated with tree names. In fact the Irish (Gaelic) word for "letter"—as well as ogham character—remains the word *fiod* (O. Ir. *fid*), which primarily means "tree." But actually the ogham system was first and foremost, and from the very beginning, a system for the bardic and Druidic *classification* of all things. Trees were of primary symbolic importance in this tradition, and so the tree names of the ogham characters became the primary or standard ones.

As "irrational" as it might seem today, the ancient Celtic wise-folk saw a secret connection between words that began with the same sound. This link, in the *heads* of the words, is a strong esoteric connection that surfaces in the poetry of the bards. In many ways this is similar to the way the Hebrew Kabbalah makes secret linkages between words which add up to the same numerical values using the system of *gematria*. There may be no logical or obvious link between them but the correspondence in sound or number points to an otherwise hidden sympathy.

Technical Oghamic Vocabulary

When talking about actual oghamic inscriptions or writing, there are certain technical terms which must be understood. The line along which the ogham characters are carved or written is called the "stemline" (O.Ir. *flesc*). Any piece of ogham writing is usually begun with a so-called "feather-sign" >, which marks the head or beginning of the writing. The marks creating the consonantal characters are referred to as "scores," while those forming the vowels are called "notches." Of course, as already mentioned, the characters themselves are actually called *fedha* (plural) or *fid* (singular), which literally means "wood" in O.Ir. An Anglicized version of this word is "few." So you may hear reference to the fews (= characters) of the ogham.

The Origins of Ogham

There are indications in the works of classical historians and ethnographers that the continental Celts used the *Greek* alphabet for certain kinds of profane written communication, but that their secret lore was not committed to writing. Caesar says (in *The Conquest of Gaul*) that the Druids believed their teachings would be profaned by being written down. This same attitude met the arrival of literacy in India at the time of Alexander—the Brahmins shunned it for the same reason. It was only later that writing was sacralized for religious and magical purposes.

It is useful to know that the Celts were using the Greek script in the last few centuries BCE, because it is clear that the

ogham is not an original system. A system such as ogham represents (essentially a code) must have an alphabetic system well-known to the encoder at work behind the scenes. The alphabetic system is the key to the numerical code represented by the ogham characters.

Also, the original alphabetic system used to create the ogham system was probably not invented for Celtic, but was a foreign alphabet adapted for use in writing Celtic. This is apparent from the fact that the H- and Z-characters are never found in ogham inscriptions in Celtic. They are, however, found on Pictish stones. (The Picts were a non-Celtic population who originally inhabited regions of present-day Scotland and who were eventually "Celticized.")

The alphabet that underlies the ogham system is probably that of the Chalcidic Greek, in use in northern Italy in the last few centuries BCE This system, shown in figure 1.2, was at some point used to write Celtic and it was probably sometime in the period between 200 BCE and 200 CE that the oghamic system was created and employed within Druidic circles on the Continent and eventually on the British Isles.

Figure 1.3: The Chalcidic Greek Alphabet

But what was the nature of the system originally? There are no ogham inscriptions on the Continent of Europe. So,

although the system probably originated there, it is unlikely that the inscribed system of scores, as we most commonly know ogham today, was in use. It is widely thought that the system was invented as a kind of sign language which Druids could use to communicate with one another secretly. This was probably a form of code using the five fingers of the hand as the basis for the code—as we see in the so-called "foot ogham" (O.Ir. *cossogam*) from *The Book of Ballymote* (Calder 1917, 296-7).

In *cossogam* the bards use the fingers of their hands in various positions along their shins to indicate the oghamic code. The fingers will be put to the right of the shinbone for the B-*aicme,* to the left for the H-*aicme,* diagonally for the M-*aicme,* and straight across for the A-*aicme.* The number of fingers used will indicate which few of the group is meant. For example, two fingers placed to the right side of the shin bone would mean the L-few.

Mythic Origins of Ogham

Just as the runes are said to have been first perceived and brought to humanity by the god Wóden, Irish sources tell us that ogham was first invented by a heroic god named Ogma. The Irish *Book of Ballymote* provides us with the following information:

> What are the place, time, person and cause of the invention of ogham? Not hard. Its place is *Hibernia insula quam nos Scoti habitamus* [The island of Hibernia, where we Scots—Irish—live]. In the time of Bres, son of Elatha [Poetic Art] king of Ireland, it was invented. Its person Ogma, son of Elatha, son of Delbaeth, brother to Bres—for Bres, Ogma and Delbaeth are the three sons of Elatha, son of Delbaeth there. Now Ogma, a man well skilled in speech and poetry, invented the ogham. The cause of its invention

was that he wanted to prove his ingenuity, and that he thought this language should belong to the learned to themselves—to the exclusion of farmers and herdsmen. Ogham got its name from Sound and Matter—who are the father and mother of ogham . . .

With respect to Sound, Ogham comes from Ogma, its inventor. But as far as Matter is concerned, *ogam* is *og-naim*— "perfect alliteration," which the bards applied to poetry. . . For the poets measure Gaelic by letters (O.Ir. *fedha*). The father of ogham is Ogma, the mother of ogham is the hand or knife of Ogma.

Moreover, this is the first thing written in ogham: ⟩ⲦⲦⲦⲦⲦⲦⲦ ; i.e., B (birch) was written (seven times) to convey a warning to Lugh, son of Ethliu. It was written about his wife, to prevent her from being abducted into the Otherworld (O.Ir. *síd*). This was seven B's on one stave (O.Ir. *flesc*) of birch. (This means): Your wife will be carried away from you seven times into the Underworld or to some other land, unless she is guarded by birch. Also, it is for this reason that B (birch) takes precedence—for it is on birch that ogham was first written.

Unfortunately, we do not have detailed myths about Ogma or how he invented the ogham system. In order to gain further insight into this god, we must go to Gaulic sources. The Greek historian Lucian (2nd century CE) reports about a fresco he saw in southern Gaul which depicted Hercules as an old, bald man leading around a troop of men by means of a chain of gold and amber running from his tongue to their ears. All of the men are smiling and happy—as is their leader. Lucian was told by a learned Gaul that the Gauls knew Hercules as *Ogmios,* and that he was shown in this form in the fresco because eloquence was considered by the Gauls to be stronger than physical strength, and that it was in fact at its peak in old age.

But oddly enough there seem to be no sign of a cult of Ogmios on the Continent. His name only appears on two curse formulas inscribed on lead plates.

Besides the passage quoted from *The Book of Ballymote,* the only other substantial reference we have to Ogma in Irish literature is found in "The Second Battle of Mag Tured," where we read that Ogma, the champion of the Tuatha Dé Danann: ". . . found Orna, the sword of Tethra, a king of the Fomorians. Ogma unsheathed the sword and cleansed it. The sword then recounted everything had been done by it—for it was the custom of swords at that time, when unsheathed, to pronounce the works that had been wrought by them." Here too there is a magical component of eloquence and perception.

The only other clues we have to myths concerning Ogma all revolve around the theme of men being led by chains attached to their leader. There is an ancient Amorican coin with this motif, and there is an obscure reference in the "Cattle-Raid of Cooley" to a man who has around his neck seven chains, to each of which are attached seven men whom he is dragging around.

It is obvious that the Irish god Ogma and the Gaulic god Ogmios are the same. What is unusual is that an apparent warrior god would govern matters of speech, eloquence and magic. But, as we have seen with the Teutonic tradition, such shifts are by no means unknown. There the god of magic, Wóden, takes on warrior characteristics.

The Use of Ogham

The ogham system is first and foremost a system of classification of things in a cosmological order—which in turn acts as a powerful aid in the process of memorization. It must be

borne in mind that the ancient Druids did not write their lore down, but rather had to commit it all to memory. The curriculum of training as a Druid may have taken as long as 20 years. Tools for the strengthening of memory were, therefore, essential to Druidic training. The intelligible ordering of things in the worlds and the ordering of words which signified these things is, on a real level, tantamount to a kind of cosmology. So the ogham system, far from being an arbitrary set of conventional signs (such as our alphabet now represents), is a complete cosmic index or guide to how things are organized in the multiverse.

In poetry, the usefulness of this system is obvious—it relates the world of sound to the world of meaning in a direct way. But the Druids were more than "just" poets. That is, "poetry" is actually a part of something much greater—which we might be tempted to call "science" today. Ogham is a system for the organization of all disciplines of thought—be they the natural sciences, magic, religion, poetry, art, medicine or law. In these disciplines, ogham enables the practitioner to classify and memorize that which he or she needs to know and have embedded deep within the soul.

How this relates to magic and divination as such should be obvious. If magic is an art and/or science of bending or twisting the natural cosmos to the will of the magician (as opposed to religion, which is the art and/or science of harmonizing one's self with the natural cosmos), then the mapping and classification of that cosmos is essential to the aims of magic (or of religion at its highest levels). Ogham is a traditionally scientific map of the cosmos. By the same token, if divination or oracular activity is the art and/or science of obtaining meaningful messages from the cosmos or spiritual structures within it, then that same cosmic map remains essential to being able not only to receive the messages but also to being able to decode them.

Besides the evidence we find in *The Book of Ballymote* and other Irish manuscripts of the Middle Ages, the other main body of evidence we have for the ogham tradition comes from ogham inscriptions themselves. These are all "memorial stones" carved to memorialize a dead man and/or to call on the gods or semi-divine ancestors of the man to help him in the Underworld. These inscriptions are not very long and they are extremely formulaic.

Ogham Inscriptions

Actual inscriptions in ogham characters are only found on the British Isles. In all, there are some 350 known ogham inscriptions, mostly carved in what is known as the Ogham Age, from about 300 to 700 CE. There appear to be only a few genuine ogham carvings later than this, although knowledge of the system passed on orally for generations before it was recorded in medieval manuscripts such as *The Book of Bally-mote*. There are some inscriptions made in the medieval period that obviously draw on the kind of knowledge preserved in the scholastic manuscripts.

Of the known ogham inscriptions, 300 are found in Ireland (mostly in the south) and the rest are on the Isle of Man and in Wales and Scotland. Most of the stones are in a Celtic dialect, of course. However, a few of the Scottish stones are perhaps Pictish—or non-Celtic—and cannot be decoded.

Most typically, an oghamic monument is a standing stone or monolith with squared or sharp edges on which the ogham is carved. These stones may have been used to mark sacred sites, but more usually they were markers of the frontiers or borders of a tribal territory.

Technically, the sharp edge of the stone would act as the stemline for the ogham, and most typically the ogham would be written from the bottom toward the top of the stone. If it continued, it would come down the adjacent edge of the stone. Rarely, the ogham characters would be carved onto the flat face of a stone (with or without an established stemline).

The contents of the inscriptions fall into two categories:

1. Memorial/Invocatory (on stones)

2. Magical (on loose objects)

The second category is not very well represented, with only a handful of examples. The first kind of inscription, however, has several subtypes. All of these could be considered "memorials," but they often seem to be calling on the dead man, his ancestors (or his gods who may be his ancestors) at the same time. In these formulas, the form N.N. stands for a name.

A. N.N.'s (stone) = This type just has the possessive form of a personal name. These are probably memorials to the dead.

B. ANM + N.N. = ANM (O.Ir. *ainm,* "name")—so this kind of inscription essentially says: "In the name of N.N.!" These are either memorials or property markers.

C. N.N. MAQI N.N. = "N.N. son of N.N." Sometimes the ANM is also prefixed. These are memorials as well.

D. N.N. AVI N.N. = "N.N. grandson (or simply descendant) of N.N." This names an ancestor more remote than the father.

E. N.N. NETA N.N. = "N.N. nephew of N.N." Here the uncle of the memorialized man is named.

F. N.N. CELI N.N. = "N.N. follower, client or devotee of N.N." Here the second name may be that of a god or a remote semi-divine ancestor.

G. N.N. MAQI MUCCOI N.N. = "N.N. son of the descendent of N.N." Here again the last name is often that of a god.

H. N.N. MAQI N.N. MAQI MUCCOI N.N. = "N.N. son of N.N. son of the descendant of N.N." —an elaborate version of type G.

K. N.N. KOI MAQI MUCCOI N.N. = "N.N. the son of the descendant of N.N." Here the dead man is identified as the preeminent or chief descendant of a divine or semidivine ancestor.

Time has not been kind to the ogham inscriptions. Because they were carved on the part of a stone most likely to suffer from the elements, they are very often so badly worn away that interpretation is difficult or impossible. But the elements were not the main enemy of the inscriptions.

Ogham may have come into use in the form of inscriptions in late pagan times, but the system as a whole and even the inscriptions themselves are features of the pagan, pre-Christian Celtic culture. As such, they appear to have been targeted for destruction by clerical thugs or devout converts to the foreign religion. There are clear traces of efforts to scrape away the oghams on many stones. In the case of those stones which probably bore the name of a Celtic god or goddess (for example, the last name on stones of types F-K) special care was taken to obliterate the name totally. Some scholars have theorized that the newly Christianized clan did this to try to cover their pagan past. The reasons remain obscure, but the fact that the stones were defaced for religious purposes seems

clear. It may have been that at certain times and places the very use of ogham itself was suspect as pagan activity, while at other times it was merely the pagan importance of divine ancestors that the clerics opposed.

Besides defacing the stones, Christians would also often try to "sanctify" or "exorcise" the stones by carving Christian crosses on them.

Actual ogham inscriptions often have irregularities of spelling and often have artificially archaic forms of language. These irregularities may have magical importance, but it must also be kept in mind that the man who actually knew ogham was perhaps not the man who actually did the carving. It may have been that one man, "a scholar" (fili), executed the ogham on a stick or on a wax tablet, and a stonemason, who was completely ignorant of ogham, was the one who actually went out into the field and carved the stone. This pattern of activity is also sometimes found in the runic culture of the Teutons.

There are indeed a number of pseudo-oghamic inscriptions (also called "plough ogham"). These are not true ogham at all, but rather superficial imitations of the script. It is thought that these represent frauds perpetrated on unsuspecting folk who paid unscrupulous oghamic con-men for memorials to their dead ancestors. It is certain that the carving of true ogham memorials was a professional activity of the old Druids—otherwise the con-men would not have been able to move in during the Christian period.

The only comprehensive edition of the ogham inscriptions is that of Macalister (1945). From his collection, we can draw a few examples to show what actual ogham inscriptions are like. Although there are not many overtly magical inscriptions, two examples can be found which are probably "words of power" inscribed onto magical objects. One is the sheep-bone from Tully Common (County Clare, Ireland). The ogham

writing on it ⟨ogham symbols⟩ can best be transcribed as "IACS." It is probably a magical formula with no meaning in natural language. The bone was probably used as a tool in magic or divination.

Another purely magical inscription is found on an amber bead which was for a long time owned by a family in the town of Ennis in the Barrony Islands. The bead is said to have healing powers and to be of help in childbirth. The inscription which runs around the bead appears:

⟨ogham inscription⟩

Macalister transliterates this: ATUCMLU, which again would be an example of a purely magical formula in ogham fews.

But apparently not only small, portable objects were inscribed with such formulas. There is also the example of the B side of the stone of Glenfahan (County Kerry, Ireland), which can be transliterated LMCBDV—again a magical formula. The Christian motifs were probably carved on later in an attempt to exorcise the stone of its pagan power.

The Stone of Glenfahan—Obverse

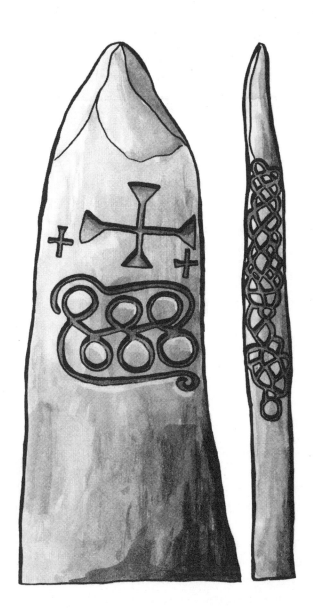

The Stone of Glenfahan—Reverse

An extraordinary example of a stone cross carved in both ogham and runes comes from Killaloe (County Clare). It was probably carved sometime in the late 1100s or early 1200s. The runes read *thurgrimristi/krusthina* ("Thorgrimr carved this cross"), and an ogham inscription which reads:

This inscription can easily be transliterated BENDACHT AR TOROQRIM, "A blessing on Thorgrim." The ogham here was probably produced by the same kind of antiquarian scholar who is responsible for the ogham sections of *The Book of Ballymote,* so this is not an inscription of the original "ogham age" but rather part of a revival of oghamic knowledge in the Middle Ages.

Far more representative of the 350 or so known ogham inscriptions is the simple formulaic "memorial" stone of Rathduff (County Kerry), which reads SIDANI MAQI DALO, "(stone) of Sidan, son of Dalo." It will also be noted that the

cross marks on the stone are again the result of later efforts to "convert" the stone and perhaps those memorialized.

Ogham in Manuscripts

No manuscripts actually written in ogham exist, although it has been thought that the "books" mentioned by classical authors referred to such records written in oghams. This is not likely; as mentioned previously, the ancient bards and Druids would not have wanted to commit their wisdom to writing. The manuscripts we are talking about here are really medieval treatises explaining the use of oghams—such as the oldest and most famous one in *The Book of Ballymote*, which dates from the 1300s. There are a number of other manuscripts containing similar tracts on the use of ogham, but they all seem derived from the same source material collected by medieval antiquarians. These various manuscripts are discussed by G. Calder in his edition of the *Auraicept na n-Eces* (1917).

Plate I on p. 23 reproduces a leaf from *The Book of Ballymote* (BB 313). Here is a translation of the Old Irish commentaries on the different figures and oghamic systems presented on that leaf as keyed to the numbers along the margin of the plate. It will be noticed that most of the long stemlines going across the whole page contain two oghamic systems each.

Translation of Leaf 313 of *The Book of Ballymote:*

43 Host ogham, i.e. the few itself to be written three times for itself, i.e. B three times, L three times, etc.

44 End to end ogham, i.e. the two ends of the stemline to be joined , i.e. group A to be mixed backwards with

group B, i.e. I between B and L, etc.; group M to be mixed with group H. The extra groups similarly.

45 Two stroke smock ogham, i.e. a stroke between every two letters in regular ogham.

46 Steadfast ogham, for its middle is the same, for there it is completed and from its latter half it is read prius, for there are the B and H groups, for in its middle is the completion of the four groups.

47 Corn field under color, there might not be two ogham fews for one few, i.e. three fews between every two fews of group B.

48 Coll, C, for a vowel, i.e. group B and group M with no change, and C for group A, five, i.e. C, CC, CCC, CCCC, CCCCC.

49 Lively dotting

50 Strife head

51 Ogham of Dedu

52 Head of dispute

53 (?)

54 Infilleted

55 Ridgeless

56 Well-footed ogham

57 Separated ogham, i.e. the fifth few is severed

58 Ebad-fashioned, i.e. an Ebad between every two fews.

59 Ogham of Fenius, i.e. the few which touches the few on its shoulder to be taken off along with it without making use of it.

60 Fraudulent ogham here, i.e. each group's defrauding another of the initial few. It is the first few of the second group (which ends the first group), ut est.

61 Side ogham of Tlachtga, i.e., on the side all these fews below.

62 (?)

63 Ogham of Eremon

64 Interwoven thread

65 Foreenclosed ogham

66 Snake through the heath

67 Angle ogham

68 (?)

69 Pierced ogham

70 (?)

71 Place ogham

72 Tooth-like ogham of Fionn, and it is for brevity that there are but two fews of every group written.

73 Shield ogham

74 Wheel ogham of Roigne Roscadach B. five, H. five, M. five, A. five.

75 Fionn's wheel

76 Stream strand of Ferchertne, i.e. five fews in each thread

77 Abbreviations

These collections and the lore contained in the medieval Irish manuscripts are not magical uses of oghams as such, but they do reflect magical uses and practices of an earlier time. These practices are usually not very well understood by the scribes and scholars collecting the material, so it is no wonder that it often appears somewhat confused and bewildering.

It is very probable that the two figures in *The Book of Bally-mote* (leaf 313) called the "Stream Strand of Ferchertne" and "Fionn's Wheel" were originally devices for the practice of magic and/or divination. Certainly they are partial cosmological maps which can be applied in these fields by those with knowledge. (See chapter 3 for an unfoldment of the mystery of Fionn's Window, for example.)

The Legacy of the Ogham-Lore

Knowledge of ogham and its intricacies died out very slowly in the Celtic realms. We know, for example, that the Earl of Glamorgan communicated with Charles I of England using ogham as a cipher in the early 1600s. But it seems that even for our old Irish scholars of the early middle ages the real mysteries of the ogham were fast being lost.

It was not until the great and enthusiastic Celtic revival beginning in the 1700s that the ogham again began to get some attention as a system which perhaps encoded actual Druidic wisdom. Unfortunately, these inspired seekers did not yet have the science at their disposal—a science that would have been very much appreciated by the ancient Druids—to unlock these mysteries. In the absence of science, poetic fancy was often substituted. Poetic fancy can be very effective when trying to conjure profound subjective experiences—many would-be magicians have been led astray by drugs in this regard. But for objective and eternal results, the hard and steadfast knowledge and truth of the oak is needed.

It has not really been until very recently that the tools necessary to recover a true and authentic oghamic lore have been at our disposal again. Centuries of ignorance and prejudice imposed by Christian belief have had to be peeled away under the light of Druidic science and analysis for the new dawn of the light emitting from within the sidhe to begin to shine again. This light has begun to illuminate such studies as that on Druidiactos by Tadhg MacCrossan, and, it is hoped, this study as well.

Chapter 2

The Runic and Oghamic Systems

In the past, writers have speculated on the possible relationship between the oghamic system and that of the Teutonic runes. Both of these systems belong to that wonderful group of writing systems which have characters bearing meaningful names. The other well-known system of this kind is the Phoenician-Semitic, best known in the form of the Hebrew alphabet. However, there does not seem to be any regular connection between or among these systems in a way that is magically significant. Each seems to have an independent existence, each representing a spiritual tradition particular to the folk who produced it: the Phoenician script for the Canaanites, the runes for the Teutons and the oghams for the Celts.

One of the main problems has been the widespread misunderstanding that the Celts used runes. Let it be said again: There is not one example of a Celtic inscription in runes. There is therefore no such thing as "Celtic runes"! The Celts had their own independent system of encoding the esoteric lore of their language and mythology, and that was the ogham system. At a late date there was an attempt on the part of at least one Briton, Nemnivus (perhaps the same as Nennius), to imitate the runes, which is discussed later, but this forms only

31

a late footnote to the runic tradition.

There are nevertheless many similarities about the ways in which runes and oghams can be used. These similarities may be the result of the long-term close contact between the Celtic and Germanic folk, especially among the chieftains, poets, magicians and merchants.

We also find a few interesting mythological parallels between the two traditions. In examining some of these briefly, we may be able to come to some deeper understandings of the workings of oghamic lore. So much more is known of the lore of the runes, and we have so many more examples of their actual use (for example, approximately 5,000 known inscriptions), that it may help to see the similarities on the innermost levels so that we can try to unlock the deepest secrets of the ogham system.

Historical Connections

The runic system may go back to about 300 BCE, or perhaps a bit further back. The oldest known runic inscription (the Meldorf brooch) dates from the middle of the first century CE, but the system must date from well before that time. It is most likely that a mixture of Roman and/or North Italic scripts acted as the models for the runic system. The runic tradition itself continued to be in use until the latter part of the 19th century in remote regions of Sweden, and it was the subject of more than one Teutonic revival. Details of the history of the runic tradition can be discovered in my *Runelore: A Handbook of Esoteric Runology* (Weiser, 1987).

It will be remembered that circumstantial evidence indicates that the ogham system may go back as far as 600 BCE among the continental Celts. (This does not necessarily imply that the methods of graphic notation in use in medieval Ireland were known that long ago.)

Throughout history, the Celts and the Teutons were interacting. During the first millennium BCE, there must have been regular and extensive contact between the Celts of the continent and the north-central European Teutons. Less well-documented, but equally probable, would be contacts between the Celts as they invaded the "British Isles" off the coast of Europe during this time.

When it comes to the deepest underlying connections between these two peoples and their religious conceptions of the cosmos, it must always be remembered that they stem from the same Indo-European source, and so both mythic and magical traditions will contain many patterns which are simply inherited from their common past.

From about 450 CE through the so-called Viking Age (800-1150), and on through the Middle Ages, the Celts and Teutons were in close contact in the British Isles and on the continent. The invasion of Britain by the Saxons in 450 led to long-term contacts in Britain, while the Viking raids and colonizations throughout the British Isles ensured close cultural contacts for several more centuries.

When we consider what the Christian response was to the pagan oghamic learning and heritage of Ireland that we learned about in the first chapter—the systematic destruction of the oghamic inscriptions—it will be understood why I say that one of the most shameful exports from Britain during the Middle Ages came in the form of evangelists. Many Irish and British Christian missionaries went to try to evangelize the Teutonic North. Not all clerics were as intolerant as their creed demanded them to be, however. Therefore, they saved some of the old pagan learning, and in this medieval form the systems of runes and oghams perhaps found their last linkage in ancient times. In the *Auraicept na N'Eces* (The scholar's primer), found in *The Book of Ballymote,* we see the following:

Juxtaposed to this it is written: *Gallogam.—Anmand na feda* ("Viking" or "foreign" ogham—names of the letters), and there follows this list of names (I have placed the actual Norse spellings of the rune names in brackets): *fea [fe], ar [ur], turs [thurs], or [oss], raid [reidh], caun [kaun], hagal [hagall], naun [naudh], isar* [actually two runes, *iss* and *ar], sol [sol], duir [tyr], bangann [bjarkan], mann [madhr], langor [logr], eir [yr].*

It is clear that the Irish scholar had some kind of genuine (if not entirely accurate) knowledge of the Scandinavian lore of his time, and that this knowledge came to him in an oral rather than written form. This is obvious from his Irish phonetic transcriptions of the names in ways other than those that would be found in written records.

Through the centuries of close cultural contact, it would be strange if the learned traditions of the Celts and those of the Teutons had not influenced each other.

The most striking similarities between the oghamic and runic traditions come in the facts that we know that both were carved on wooden staves for divinatory purposes and that both used a kind of number-pairing code. An explanation of this would be that the ogham characters were first numerals on tallysticks, which were later used for mnemonic purposes. This is the shared feature that has set most serious scholars wondering about the connections between these two traditions. The difference is that ogham *is* one of these systems, while the runes can be *transformed* into one of them. A discussion of these runic codes can be found in chapter 7 of my book, *Runelore.*

In order to show how similar runic codes are to the oghamic system, it is necessary to show an example of how the rune-codes work. The runic system is always divided into three families or groups *(ættir)* just as the oghams are divided into *aicme.* In the Viking Age, the runic system consisted of 16 runestaves arranged in three groups. For purposes of encoding, the groups were even rearranged so that what normally would have been the first group is the third—or, looking at it another way, the aett-order was reversed. The system would appear:

Ætt	Runestave					
	1	2	3	4	5	6
1	t	b	m	l	R	
2	h	n	i	a	s	
3	f	u	th	a	r	k

With this system, any rune can be represented with two numbers. For example, 3/2 = u; that is, the third group, second rune is the u-rune. This could be expressed graphically as:

Rune-codes became a learned game in the Scandinavian Middle Ages, but originally they had the magical purpose of further concealing the runic meanings—thus making their effect more powerful.

One historical example of the code-runes is found in the rock of the Maeshowe burial chamber in the Orkney Islands. These date from the late 1100s and read as shown on the following page:

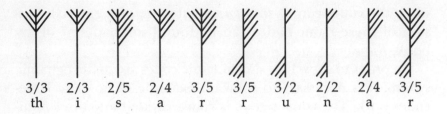

| 3/3 | 2/3 | 2/5 | 2/4 | 3/5 | 3/5 | 3/2 | 2/2 | 2/4 | 3/5 |
| th | i | s | a | r | r | u | n | a | r |

That is: *thisar runar,* "these runes."

The graphic principle of rune-codes is simple: represent two numbers (1-3 for the ættir and 1-5 or 6 for the runestave in that particular aett) and you have written a secret rune.

Many more examples of these runic codes are discussed in the book *Runica Manuscripta* by Rene Derolez (1954).

It can be seen why scholars have been arguing over the relationship between these systems when the techniques of runic codes are considered.

An odd but significant sidelight to the history of the relations between the runes and the Celtic world is the story of the alphabet of Nemnivus (who may be the same a Nennius who wrote the *History of the Britons).* This alphabet was invented by Nemnivus in the early 800s based on the Old English runic Futhorc. It is said that he invented them because he was confronted by a learned Saxon who chided the Britons for not having a true set of their own letters. The table of the Nemnivus Alphabet at the end of this book shows how he used not only the runic shapes but the names as well.

The God of the Runes and the Magical Gods of the Celts

It is very well known that the Teutonic God Wóden (or Ódhinn) is the runic God *par excellence.* Wóden is the high

God of the Teutonic folk, as well as being the chief God of poetry, magick, death—and eventually of war and sovereignty. Ódhinn won—or took up—the runes as a result of an initiatory ordeal described in the Eddic poem entitled the "Hávamál"—or Sayings of the High One (who is none other than Ódhinn himself). Note that it is not said that Ódhinn "invented" the runes, but rather he found something that already existed in the objective universe—the universal mysteries (runes). Throughout the lore surrounding the runes, Ódhinn is described as and shown to be the God of the runes and the God of the Runemasters.

In Celtic lore, the invention of ogham is ascribed to the God Ogma. (This myth is outlined on pp. 11-12 in chapter 1.) Ogma is said to have invented ogham. Ogham is therefore not to be equated with the mysteries or secrets it might encode. In the science of comparative religion and mythology, Ogma is most characterized as a warrior god. That the Celtic Hercules is the inventor of a form of secret writing is seen as a statement concerning the absolute power of this kind of writing, which goes beyond any profane or mundane function.

Ogham is a system of classification of all things based on the mystery of sounds arranged in a certain order. It is according to this principle that oghamic lists—which appear to be little more than word-lists arranged according to their initial letters—can be arranged. The runes are based on the mysteries themselves—a certain arrangement and ordering of ideas or principles—of which sounds, words, shapes and so forth are visible manifestations. Once the distinction is grasped, the enormous differences between the two systems will be understood. Each possesses its own unique purpose and genius. They are not interchangeable.

Besides Ogma, other Gods or figures from Celtic lore might be connected with a function similar to that held by

Ódhinn among the Teutons. Comparative mythologists have shown that the religious systems ultimately branching off from the Indo-European stock contain Gods and Goddesses which correspond to one another on extremely deep levels. The best historian of religion to look at this for the Celts was Jan de Vries, whose German-language work *Keltische Religion* (1961) is a classic.

Greatest among the Celtic analogs to Ódhinn is the Irish Tuatha Dé Danann God called *Lugh Lamfadha*—the "Long Armed." De Vries identifies no less than nine strong correspondences between them. Both:

1. are chief Gods (Lugh is known as the High God of the Gauls)

2. are war-leaders

3. play leading roles in the ancient battle between two primeval races of gods (Ódhinn in that between the Æsir and Vanir, Lugh in the battle of Mag Tured)

4. have spears as their weapons

5. use magic in battle and elsewhere

6. employ a single-eyed magical technique (Lugh closes one eye, while Ódhinn actually sacrifices one)

7. are masters of poetry

8. are connected with ravens

9. are the progenitors of heroes (most notably Sigurd by Ódhinn and CúChulainn by Lugh).

Although it is generally the policy of this book to concentrate on Irish evidence as much as possible, as it is in Irish that we have the bulk of the true oghamic evidence, in this comparative chapter we will delve a bit into the Cymric (Welsh) material. (Here we prefer to use the actual term for "Welsh"—Cymric—as Welsh is really a Teutonic way of saying "people of confused speech," or barbarians.)

The Cymric form of Lugh is Lleu, who appears in the Fourth Branch of the *Mabinogi* ("Math Son of Mathonwy"). Beyond this Lleu, however, the Cymric legend provides us with two other interesting figures who correspond to the Teutonic God of the runes on some level: Gwydion and Merlin (Cymric Myrddin). Some hold that the very name of Gwydion is related to that of Ódhinn—and that both are derived from the Indo-European root *wat-*, magico-poetic inspiration. This may or may not be so. But more certainly Cymric *gwawd* means the poetic art, just as the Old Norse word *ódhr* can mean the same thing. Gwawdd is related to the Celtic *uatis,* seer, and to the Irish word *faith,* prophet. Merlin is the Cymric magician *par excellence,* who also corresponds to many of the Odinic functions.

The academic question of whether ogham influenced the runes, or if the reverse is the case, is irrelevant to the ultimate unraveling of the mysteries of either system. Both systems, as we have them now and as they were used in ancient times, constitute vital independent traditions that are most meaningful within their own contexts. Infecting one system with the other, or bringing in even more exotic systems such as Hebrew Kabbalah, would only serve to obscure what is genuine within the tradition at hand. In the history of spiritual revival movements, it often happens that the basic underlying structures—the true soul of traditions—go undetected while better known and obvious structures from outside traditions are applied to the myths and legends—so that the overall effect is one of exotic Gods in traditional clothing. What do you have if you put Yahweh in a kilt? An inappropriately dressed

Hebrew storm god. The same can be said for trying to fit the oghamic tradition into the runic, or either into the Kabbalistic. Interesting things can be learned from such games, but primary efforts should be spent where the richest results will be yielded—within the tradition. If everything is everything, then nothing is anything.

Chapter 3

Cosmology and Divination

The key to any divinatory system is to be found in the cosmology of which the system is a product. Questions of how the world came to be (cosmogony) and how it is organized (cosmology) are essential, as are the questions of how the system being used in divination fits into these models. In order to learn how the ancients thought, we must learn of their cosmogony, cosmology, psychology and theology—that is, how they thought the world came to be, how it is structured now, how they related to it spiritually and what greater forces are at work in this world (or worlds). This gives the context for understanding the ancient and timeless levels of wisdom contained in the mythic thought of the ancestors.

Cosmogony

The Birth of the World

We have no straightforward account of the cosmology or cosmogony of the ancient Celts, although we can assume from the later evidence that they did indeed have sophisticated ideas on these subjects. The widely used cosmological material from the so-called *Barddas* created in the early 1800s by Iolo Morganwg is based directly on Neo-Platonic ideas and has no close link with the genuine ideas concerning the shape of the world or Celtic lore on how it came into being. We must therefore look again to the source for the answers to the essential questions.

Although the Irish largely "historicized" their mythology— perhaps in an attempt to be able to preserve the structures of their ancient tradition without making it subject to total rejection by the incoming Christian ideology. A myth that talks of the Gods and Goddesses as if they were humans would be much more likely to survive editings and re-editings by generations of Christian monks.

This is apparently what happened with the cosmology. In the *Lebor Gabála Érenn* (Book of the invasions of Ireland), we read that the island was invaded five times before the coming of the "Sons of Mil"; that is, the Gaelic folk. In the tale of these five invasions, the Irish tradition seems to have preserved the substance of a mythic cosmogony in which five waves of essential being are poured out over an originally formless mass, giving it shape and existence. The people of Cessair lived on the island before the deluge and did not "divide," or shape the land. The second invasion was that of the Partholon, who divided the land by four. In so doing they created a flat plane—the four quarters—on which life could emerge. The third invasion was that of the Nemed, who divided the land by three. In doing this they gave a spiritual or vertical dimension to reality. The fourth invasion was that of the Fir Bolg. These folk divided the land into "fifths." This synthesizes the four and the three in a new whole model of reality. The Tuatha Dé Danann, who were the fifth wave of invaders, bring in an entirely new dimension of spirituality which defies the laws of the world of three dimensions. Finally, the Gaelic folk invade and divide the land into two halves—an upper and a lower (north and south)—while at the same time accepting the five-fold division instituted by the Fir Bolg. The twofold division is a recognition of the duality of the cosmos as we (as human beings) experience it—the light and the dark, the male and the female, the inside and outside etc.—of virtually everything we experience in the world.

The land of Ireland is shown to be a kind of *prima materia* onto which the emanations of being are projected over time, giving rise to the world as we know it—here symbolized by the island of Eriu. The original way of expressing this cosmogonic process may have been quite different from what we have now, but at the same time it was probably structurally similar to the account of how Ireland came into being. For in the traditional mind all things come into being along similar patterns or laws, whether it is the whole cosmos or one corner of it. In the Indo-European ideology, every time new land is taken, the world is created (or recreated) in the act.

The Celtic Cosmology

Again the Celtic sources present some problems for the modern seeker for the esoteric secrets of the ancient Druids.

On the one hand, the sources of Celtic myth and legend are extremely rich in detailed accounts of journeys to the Otherworld and the Underworld (or otherworlds), but, on the other hand, the sources are very unsystematic about describing what obviously had a sophisticated system at one point. This is understandable to some extent due to the Christianization process. The heart and soul of a spiritual tradition is housed in its cosmological and psychological lore. These, therefore, were the first areas to be most obscured by Christian re-editings of the mythic texts. Modern comparative studies have, however, provided the keys necessary to unlock the obscure texts that were left behind.

When you read the Celtic legend and lore, you are always struck by the omnipresence of the Otherworld. At any time, in the most unexpected places, the Otherworld can break through the veil of this existence and envelop a hero. The Celtic Otherworld is a concept that comes very close to the ideas of "neo-physicists" regarding the presence of other geometrical dimensions coexisting in a parallel universe with our own reality of three dimensions.

The words "Otherworld" and "Underworld" must be kept distinct. In the Celtic cosmology—or map of the whole of existence as it is right now—there are three levels of types of reality. First there is that of this world (O.Ir. *bith*), which is the realm of three dimensions in space and motion (= time). There is also an-Otherworld—actually Otherworld*s*—which can symbolically be thought to be "above" this one. Its symbolic height is really a reflection of a higher dimensionality. It is a parallel universe coexisting with this one. It is difficult to reach—but it may be reached through hidden doorways into this realm which may appear anywhere. The most common apertures into this Otherworld are through ancient burial mounds or at sacred wells or trees. The third world is the

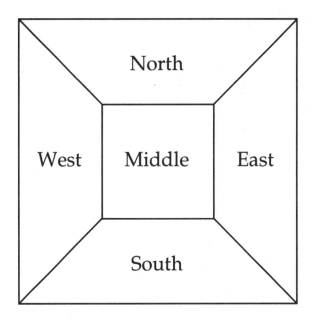

Figure 3.1: The Fifths

Underworld, which is symbolically very distant from this world. It is symbolized as being far to the west and/or under the sea.

This division of the universe into three realms, one above and one below this one, appears to be a common trait of Indo-European cosmology. (For a comparison to the Teutonic cosmology, see my *Runelore*, chapter 10.)

Although no exact number is ever ascribed to the worlds, it is likely that the Celts originally had a nine-world system, as this number figures so prominently in their cosmologies. But of primary importance would be the number five—which represents the "provinces" or fifths (O.Ir. *coiced*) into which all territory is divided. This pattern is one of four outer realms, with a fifth in the mystical center (O.Ir. *Mide*). The mystical center

is the gateway for the entry of influence of the Otherworlds into this world.

The five *forfedha*, or "additional letters," of the oghamic system have a special significance in the cosmology. They are either latecomers to the system of writing or stand somewhat outside it. These fews are not the same kind of signs as the others; they are truly symbols, carrying with them shapes that suggest their cosmological—and hence divinatory—significance. They have certain meanings within themselves as signs of the cosmic Fifths, and they show how that Fifth relates to the sovereign center. Each *forfedha* can be seen to correspond in meaning to one of the Fifths, as shown in figure 3.2., and as incorporated into the design of the casting cloth.

The ea-few is right in the center of the diagram as a symbol of the absolute middle of the cosmos defined by crossed lines. The cosmological meanings of all the *forfedha* are shown in table 3.1, which can be compared to the lore contained in table 1.1 in chapter 1.

Table 3.1: The Cosmological Meanings of the Forfedha

Shape	Sound	Direction	Field	Meaning
	ae	east	blath	manifestation
	io	north	cath	conflict–resistance
	ui	west	fis	learning–spiral
	oi	south	seis	harmony–space
	ea	center	mide	middle–focus

Remember that this table unfolds from the bottom upwards.

Figure 3.2: The Forfedha in the Fifths

The *forfedha* describe a spiraling unfoldment from the X point in the middle to a space or opening ◇ in which manifestation can take place, moving in a spiraled ◎ or cyclical fashion, meeting resistance and conflict ※ and finally coming to a completed matrix of manifestation in the grid pattern of the world ⊞ .

Through a careful analysis of the names given to the various Otherworlds and Underworlds of the ancient Irish, an original system has been reconstructed which probably comes close to the original. The term *magh* (plane) is usually given to supernal Otherworlds, while the term *tír* (land) is ascribed to Underworldly realms.

The upper world, or Otherworld, can be described with the generic Old Irish term *Magh Mor* (the Great Plane), while the Underworld can be called by the general term *Tír Ando-main* (the Land of the Un-world, or Anti-World). But it can also simply mean "lowlands" in Irish. Each of these two realms, along with this world *(Bith)* in the middle, can be divided into four outer provinces or cosmic realms. *Magh Mor* is divided into four realms indicative of (1) age, (2) light, (3) abundance, and (4) happiness, while *Tír Andomain* is likewise divided into four realms indicative of (1) youth, (2) love, (3) vitality and (4) death. Into *Bith* all these influences flow.

Table 3.2: The Realms in Celtic Cosmology

The Upper- or Otherworld *(Magh Mor)*		
Name	**Translation of Name**	**Quality**
1 *Sen Magh*	Old Plain	(age)
2 *Magh Findargat*	Plain of White Silver	
Magh Imchiunn	Plain of Extreme Gentleness	(light)
Magh Argetnel	Plain of Silver Clouds	
3 *Magh Mell*	Plain of Delight	
Magh Aircthech	Plain of Bounty	(abundance)
Magh Ildathach	Plain of Many Colors	
4 *Magh Ionganaidh*	Plain of Wonder	(happiness)
The Middle World *(Bith* or *Mide)*		
The Under- or Anti-world		
1 *Tír na n'Óg*	Land of Youth	(growth)
2 *Tír fo Thuinn*	Land under the Wave	(death)
Tech Duinn	House of Donn	
3 *Tír na mBan*	Land of Women	(love)
4 *Tír na mBeo*	Land of Life	(vitality)

There is one common name for the Underworld, *Tír Tairngiri* (the Land of Promise—or the Promised Land), which is an obvious borrowing from the Christian tradition, and so its possible implications have been ignored for purposes of reconstructing the actual Celtic conceptions.

When the whole is put together, the structure resembles a tree—which is the support structure for the entire system of worlds, realms and provinces—as shown in Figure 3.3 on page 50.

When this structure is envisioned, a network of paths or streams interconnecting these realms and worlds also appears, and, amazingly, they can be seen to be 20 in number. This is, of course, the same as the number of the fews of the ogham system. Here the idea of the trees being means of mysto-magical access to the powers of other worlds becomes more obvious and practical.

The Oghamic Reflection in the Cosmos

In *The Book of Ballymote* we find a puzzling figure called Fionn's Window (see p. 25 above). The exact meaning of this figure may be revealed when it is used as an instrument for analyzing—for clearly envisioning—the Celtic cosmology according to oghamic principles. Fionn's Window consists of five rings, each inscribed with four ogham characters. If the two dimensional "window" is projected or unfolded into three-dimensional space, the five groups of ogham-fews can be seen to form levels of the great cosmic tree, as shown in figure 3.4 on page 51.

In this way, ogham-fews are ascribed to each of the 20 paths in the cosmological scheme. The single-stroke fews

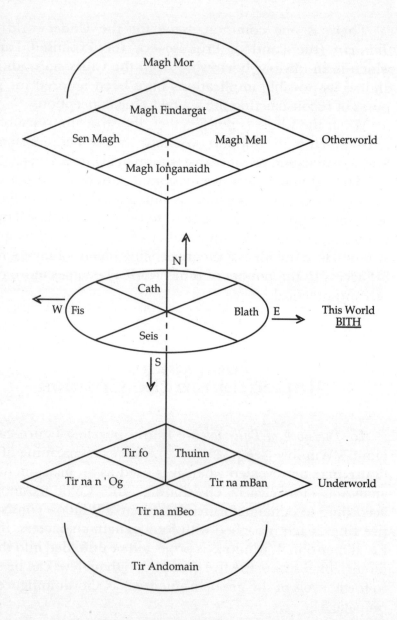

Fig 3.3: The Celtic Cosmology

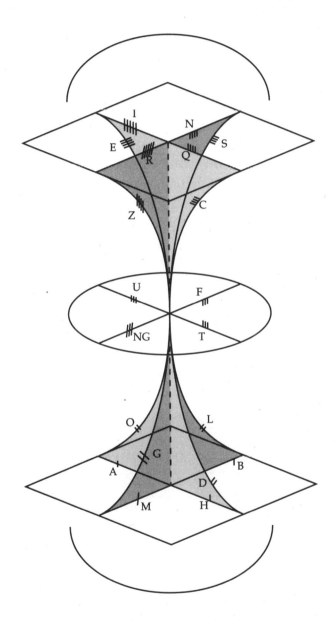

Figure 3.4: The Ogham-Fews in the Celtic Cosmology

belong to the Underworld plane, the double-stroke fews to the paths of access to the Underworld, the triple-stroke characters to this plane of existence, the quadruple- stroke fews to the paths of access to the Otherworld and finally the quintuple-stroke characters to the plane of the Otherworld itself.

The mysterious central axis does not itself make up any of these paths—for the paths are means of human access to the Otherworlds, while the direct vertical axis would be the means of influence on this world from the Otherworlds.

It will also be noted that there are symbolic directions indicated on the cosmological map in figure 3.3, and in the middle of each of the "lands," "fifths," or "plains" there is a point. Each of these points represents one of the four "Otherworldly cities" of Irish tradition. The fact that all four are represented on all three levels of being simultaneously shows the interaction of these "places" or states of being throughout the depth and breadth of the entire cosmos. Their names, symbolic locations, masters and basic meanings are shown in Table 3.3. It should be noted that the "masters" are clearly a later Christian addition.

Table 3.3: The Otherworldly Cities

Name	Direction	Master	Symbol
Falias	North	Morfessa	Stone
Gorias	East	Esras	Spear
Finias	South	Uscias	Sword
Murias	West	Semias	Cauldron

When the whole is seen, there are nine realms, arrayed through three worlds, divided into a total of 12 provinces—all interconnected by 20 paths or streams. The universe is seen to have essentially three levels of being, each divided into "fifths"—a hidden or invisible center and four external provinces around it.

When all of this is reprojected onto a flat surface for purposes of divination or the playing of sacred games meant to mirror the possible happenings within the whole cosmos, the pattern of the "fifths," on which the divinatory cloth is based emerges. This whole cosmic scheme is also the pattern underlying the so-called Celtic cross.

Theories of Divination

Divination is the art and practice of gaining hidden knowledge, especially when it is derived from divine or objective sources. Historically in the Celtic world, this was done in a wide variety of ways. The oghams were just one of many methods used to divine the hidden reality behind the world of appearances. As far as most of the other methods are concerned, they are unfortunately so obscure as to how the objective symbolic meanings were understood that they have been totally lost to any accurate or reliable reconstruction. The ogham system, on the other hand, is well enough documented and enough of its true symbology has survived intact so that we can still understand the essence of how it worked. This understanding has been put into practice in this system of ogham divination.

The aim of divination is basically to set up a meaningful dialog with the universe—both within the inquirers and between the individual inquirers and their universe. Divination is a way of learning things that otherwise would be hidden from the awareness of the diviner. Among ancient peoples this knowledge could just as often involve the roots of things—the hidden history of a person or place—as it would the as yet unseen branches in the "yet to be." The reason for this is that the ancient Indo-Europeans—including the Celts and Teutons—deeply understood that the so-called "future" or the "fate" of a person or place is strongly linked to the past of that person or place. If the past if fully and deeply understood the "future" can be predicted with some accuracy.

This idea is very clear in the various narratives in Old Irish literature which refer to the vital necessity of knowing the history of Ireland. For example, we read in *The Book of Invasions* about the primeval figure Fintan son of Bochra (= Ocean), daughter of Bith (= World), who survived all upheavals of the world (often living in a cave in the shape of a salmon) and who was summoned to recount the history of the land so that the men of Ireland would know how to divide the land rightly. The recurrence of the "salmon of knowledge" theme is constant in Celtic lore. The salmon represents the primeval understanding of the basis of existence. Knowledge of this seed principle makes all knowledge possible.

For divination to be true or real, it must be knowledge derived from objective sources. The main role of tradition in this inner process is the establishment of authentic and accurate methods of deriving this knowledge. It is possible for people to delude themselves into believing they have gained profound knowledge through wholly subjective means. In this procedure, however, it is all too easy to produce the sensation of meaningfulness devoid of all objective significance. The ancients understood this well, and this is why they are always so insistent on the derivation of their knowledge from true primeval sources. So too must it be today for us to seek and find true mysteries on our chosen paths.

There are generally two main types of divination, an objectified type and a subjective type. As in all systems in which meaning is derived, both are essentially made up of two symbol systems which are synthesized to arrive at a given meaning.

Examples of the objectified systems would be those connected to the runes, astrology, tarot cards and so forth. In these systems, one set of symbols (for example the zodiacal signs in astrology) are juxtaposed or laid over another set of symbols (the houses in astrology). The same pattern is used in rune casting or laying tarot cards. All of these take an essentially rational approach to the subject, and from the firm rational basis apply intuitive skill to interpret the synthesis—the meaningful melding—of the two symbols.

The best modern example of the subjective method is seen in the currently fashionable practice of "channeling." In this technique the diviners meld their minds (or verbal segments of it) with an inner (or outer) source of information. This is a method known within the Teutonic school of *seith,* and among the Irish similar techniques were known as *imbas forosna* (inspiration from the knowledge of the masters) and *dichetal do chennaib* (composing on the fingertips) or extemporary incantation.

In virtually all kinds of divination. we see that two systems of meaning are synthesized, bought together, to result in an expanded interpretation of the symbols which go beyond the obvious into some otherwise hidden realm of significance. This way of working is not as extraordinary as it might at first appear. After all, our everyday language and its common understanding is based on this same principle. We use words, which are placed in certain meaningful positions in a context (sentence) in order to derive some meaning from the words. Each word has a meaning, but, in the overall context of a sentence, it acquires more significance and may sometimes change its meaning entirely based on where it appears in a sentence.

In many ways, divinatory systems work on the same principles. This is why they can so easily be referred to as *metalanguages*. They work much the same as natural languages do, but they signify something beyond the ordinary natural symbol systems. They must be interpreted by a higher faculty of the soul in order for them to be reliably used. In using a divinatory metalanguage, the bards are virtually having conversations with their environments.

With the ogham system, the ogham fews constitute the "words" of the metalanguage, while the various patterns found in the cosmic order and in the locations of meaning in all the layouts make up the "sentences" or contexts in which these complex symbols can be understood and interpreted.

The Celtic View

In the Celtic world, ogham is not the only kind of divination known. If we look at the other kinds of divination, we will certainly better understand the nature and uses of the oghamic form.

In the ancient Celtic sources, there are many different methods mentioned for gaining hidden knowledge. There were methods involving the induction of prophetic dreams, as well as those for drawing out inspired utterances of prophesy from within the bard through poetry.

The induction of prophetic dreams is known in Old Irish by such terms as *tarbfeis* ("bull-feast") and *taghairm*. The *tarbfeis* involved the eating of the flesh and drinking the blood of a correctly sacrificed bull and sleeping wrapped up in its still-warm hide. This was done for the special purpose of inducing a dream to determine the identity of the future king. The

taghairm simply had the diviner wrapped up in the warm hide of a freshly sacrificed ox. The seer then slept in this hide in a remote location until prophetic dreams were induced.

In a work called "Cormac's Glossary" *(Sanas Cormaic)* we read of three distinct types of divination practiced by the ancient Irish: *imbas forosnai* ("revelation of knowledge"), *teinem laida* ("cracking [or analysis] of a poem"), and *dichtetal do chennaib* ("extemporary incantation").

The *imbas forosnai* involves the chewing of raw meat of a sacrificial animal. The meat is offered to the Gods while incantations are sung over the diviner's hands. The diviner then goes to sleep covering his eyes with his hands—the right palm over the left eye, and the left palm over the right eye. The dreams will reveal the desired knowledge.

Teinm laida, like *imbas forosnai,* was connected with sacrifice and the invocation of the old Gods of the people. For this reason both were strictly prohibited by the Christians. With "cracking open" or analysis of a situation poetically, the diviner composes a poetic work to find the answer to a question.

The form of divination called *dichtetal do chennaib* apparently is based on the mind and abilities of the diviner alone with no outside help from the Gods or sacrificial acts.

One recurring ritual element in the Celtic tradition is that of the *det fis*—the Tooth of Knowledge. In the Irish tradition, Fionn mac Cumhaill is said to possess this. In one story, Fionn gets his thumb caught in a door jamb, and in another he touches his thumb to a cooking salmon ("the Salmon of Knowledge"). In both cases, he puts the injured digit in his mouth to relieve the pain and is suddenly gifted with prophetic insight. There is also a parallel to this in Teutonic tradition In the *Saga of the Volsungs,* we read of Sigurd gaining divinatory powers when he burns his finger on the bubbling heart-blood of the serpent, Fafnir, and similarly puts his finger in his mouth. In these cases, it is the magical connection to the praeterhuman realm (embodied in the salmon or serpent), coupled with a spontaneous, synchronistic "accident," which provides the impetus for the new unfoldment of powers.

Since the oghams are first and foremost a system of classifying and cataloging in a complete and significant way all aspects of the world and environment, to the traditional Celtic mind the oghams would make up a complete set of symbols existing within the natural cosmic order. To read where and how these aspects are working at any one time in a person's life is one of the chief things such a system makes possible. To continue with our linguistic analogy, the complete ogham system is the dictionary, while the cosmology is the *grammar* of the metalanguage. This goes a long way towards explaining the true significance of why the treatises on ogham go on and on about the various "kinds" of ogham. It is simply an effort to expand and refine the "dictionary" of symbolic meanings in order that the universe might be more accurately understood and interpreted.

In ogham the language itself is imbued with hidden meaning. In the original tradition, ogham was a science of language, and language was seen as a magical way to interact with the cosmos. Ogham divination as outlined here is the uncovering of the basic principles in this system and their use in a meaningful dialog between the self and the world.

Chapter 4

The Soul

In order to understand how the world interacts with the individual, we need to understand just what makes up that individual. Since we are using a traditional "metalanguage"—the oghams of the Celts—to map the objective universe, to be harmonious it is best to use the traditional Celtic psychology to map the internal or subjective world as well.

Psychology—or more simply *soul-lore*—along with cosmology interact to give us profound ways to understand ourselves and the world. The more we know about the workings of the inner world, the better we can know and predict things about events in the outer world.

The subject of traditional Celtic psychology is well covered in Tadhg MacCrossan's *Sacred Cauldron*. What I want to focus on here is the way in which the soul-parts are used by the bard in working with oghamic divination or other forms of magic.

First it must be understood that the Celts, like all Indo-European peoples, had a refined "poly-psychic" concept of how the psychosomatic (soul-body) complex was made up. This could be compared to the way the Germanic soul-conceptions are outlined in my *Book of Troth* (1989, 89-102) and *Runelore* (1987, 167-173). Neither of these systems is unique, however All the Indo-European psychological systems had similar structures. Each system is in harmony with the folk-group it describes or expresses.

Nowadays, the average person is rather impoverished when it comes to having a language to describe precisely what is going on in the inner life. The ancient Celts had a richer and more exacting language to express these psychological states and essences. This language was not a matter of academic or "scientific" learning (such as our modern and rather artificial psychoanalytic terminologies). For them it was a matter of experience and expression of that experience in an appropriate symbolic language. The language expressed the common experience or extraordinary states of consciousness. This stands in sharp contrast to modern English as spoken by the average speaker today, who is not very much aware of the exact distinctions between such terms as spirit, mind, soul, psyche or intellect.

When we look at the ancient Irish soul-conceptions, we can see seven distinct entities:

1. The appearance or shape *(delbh)*

2. The elements *(duile)* which make up The body

3. The animating principle or breath *(anál)*

4. The mind and will *(menma)*

5. The memory *(cuimhne)*

6. The self *(féin)*

7. The shadow or shape-shifting form *(púca* or *scal)*

8. The shade or soul *(enaid)*

In many ways, a reading of the ogham fews in a divinatory working is a matter of reading or interpreting the synthesis or

interaction of these factors of the soul with the map of the world.

1. The *delbh* [delv] is the image or outer form of the person. This is a malleable substance. Actors and magicians are usually experts at altering this aspect of themselves. This is not the physical vehicle itself but rather the subtle shell which the physical elements, or duile, fulfill.

2. The *duile* [duiluh] are made up of six elements of the human vehicle or microcosm, each of which corresponds to an element in the macrocosm:

Human	World
anál (breath)	*gaeth* (wind)
imradud (mind)	*nel* (cloud)
drech (face)	*grain* (sun)
fuil (blood)	*muir* (sea)
colaind (flesh)	*talamh* (earth)
cnaimh (bone)	*cloch* (stone)

These elements are arranged in a descending order of density. The presence of the spiritual breath concept and the mind show that the ancient Celts may have known what we now guess to be certain gateways in the psychosomatic, or soul-body, complex that link the functions of what we have historically called the "spiritual" and "physical" realms.

3. the *anál* [anahl], although part of the *duile,* must also be considered as a separate category because of its position as the animating and vitalizing principle. It is not an intellectual or cognitive principle, but rather a purely vitalistic one—in it the

life-force is carried into the rest of the body and through it the individual vitality can influence the outside world.

4. The *menma* [MEN-mah] is the combined cognitive and volitive mental capacities—it is the seat of thought and the will. That these two faculties are so closely linked under a single term indicates the level of unity between them in the Celtic mind.

5. The *cuimhne* [kuv-nuh] is the precise faculty of memory. In some ways is may be thought to be subordinate to, or another part of, the *menma,* but, as the faculty of memory is so important to the practice of the oghamic arts, it is fitting that there be a separate term for it in the language.

6. The *féin* [fane] (self) is the centralized vehicle of individual consciousness. It is in and through the *féin* that the individual is known in, and comes to know, the world in which he or she lives.

7. The *púca* [pooka] is the shadow side of the personality. It can be a dangerous or unsettling aspect to become aware of at the wrong time or under bad circumstances. The púca is itself a divine part of a person—but an often tricky or terrifying aspect of divinity. It can almost be an alternate persona— often used for magical or martial purposes. How often have we heard of a star football player that "he becomes another person, like a wild-man on the field, but off the field he is as gentle as a lamb"? Such are the púca-like manifestations.

8. The *enaid* [inathe] is the shadow or shade manifestation which is only apparent upon the death of a person. It is that part of a person which shows or makes known certain aspects of the person's life when he or she dies.

The overall structure of how these various soul conceptions

fit together to shape the whole of a person in the Celtic tradition is shown in figure 4.1. To understand and form a general feeling for how the various parts of the psyche work together— or sometimes at odds with each other !—is necessary not only to gain an intuitive understanding of how the ancient Celts thought and felt—but more directly such understanding will greatly aid in reading oghamic fews in divinatory acts.

Rebirth of the Soul

It is often said that the ancient Celts believed in "reincarnation." This is not true if by "reincarnation" it is meant that the psyche—including personal memories—was thought to be transferred from a dead person to the unborn in an arbitrary fashion. The idea that a Celtic chieftain could be "reborn" as a Roman soldier or an Indian potter would have been unthinkable. But they—along with all their fellow Indo-Europeans—did hold that the essential powers and abilities of the dead were almost genetically passed on to their descendants and relatives within the tribe or clan. This genetic chain reaches all the way back to the Gods and Goddesses themselves. The descendants are the ancestors reborn. As the ancient Celts were not as alienated from the reality of their bodies as modern people often are, the idea that the descent of the body from one form to another was paralleled by a spiritual descent was only natural—and so it will be again.

The ogham inscriptions themselves discussed in chapter 1 give good evidence of the importance not only of genetic lines of descent, but also the linkage of that line with the quasi-physical reality of the Gods.

Classical authors mentioned a belief in immortality held by

the Celts. The Greek ethnographer Poseidonios was probably the original source for most of these early references. He equated the Celtic doctrine with that of the Greek philosopher Pythagoras. Julius Caesar probably used Poseidonios as his source when he wrote:

> A lesson which they [the druids] take particular pains to inculcate is that the soul does not perish, but after death passes from one body to another; they think this is the best incentive to bravery, because it teaches men to disregard the terrors of death.
>
> —*De bello Gallico* VI, 14

A series of authors, including Diodorus Siculus, Strabo and Lucanus, wrote similar ideas concerning the Celtic conceptions of life after death and rebirth. The purpose for most of these classical authors' statements was an explanation of the lack of fear the Celts displayed in battle. It is not clear what direct evidence these authors had for these beliefs.

The most reliable evidence we have comes from the oldest literatures of Ireland, Scotland and Wales, along with comparative evidence from cultures closely related with the Celtic.

Within the corpus of Irish literature there are three main cycles containing rebirth motifs: those of Etain, CúChulainn and Finn.

In the Etain cycle, we find what is perhaps the best example of the concept, because the tale spans three generations of rebirths. The third of these is the daughter of the second, and they all bear the same name. On the surface, this can be somewhat confusing to the reader of these tales—but the meaning conveyed is most profound. Originally Etain is divine. She is the wife of the God Midir in the *sídhe*-mound (or Otherworld). Subsequently, she is incarnated as Etain, the daughter of Etar, king of Echrad. In this form, she marries Eochaid,

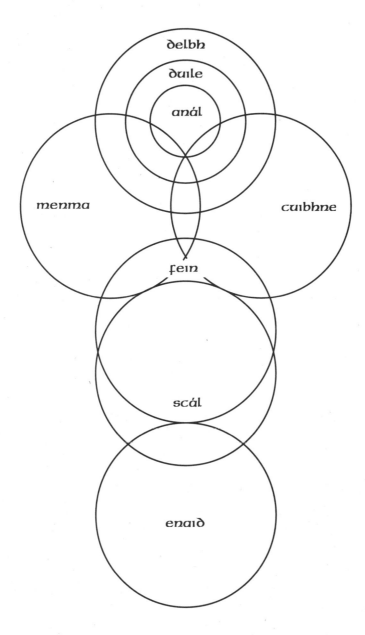

Figure 4.1: Diagram of the Celtic Soul Concept

king of Tara. Etain, the wife of Eochaid, then bears one daughter, also named Etain.

The CúChulainn cycle presents us with a classic example of the divine ancestor. After an interlude of three years in the Otherworld, Dechtire bears a son named Setanta. The God Lugh is the actual father of the boy, although Sualtach, the mortal husband of Dechtire, claims him.

CúChulainn always remains conscious of his divine origin. This motif is the most common found in the Irish rebirth tales—a divine member of the Otherworld and one of the Tuatha Dé Danann is the father of a "mortal" child and at the same time is thought to be "incarnated" in the child. (This follows from the basic idea that the descendants are the ancestors reborn.) Of course, the God continues to exist in the Otherworld while his "avatar" (to use a Sanskrit word for a similar conception) acts in this world.

The CúChulainn cycle also provides an example of another feature of the Celtic rebirth ideology separate from the influence of the Otherworld. In the tale called "The Wooing of Emer," CúChulainn's countrymen (the Ulstermen) are anxious that their champion and hero marry and produce an heir as soon as possible because of their fear that he would perish early. They wished for this heir "knowing that his rebirth (O.Ir. *aithgain)* would be of himself." This can easily be compared to the third rebirth of Etain.

The third primary example of this teaching in Irish literature is found in the "Voyage of Bran" and other later Irish tales dealing with Mongan. King Fiachna is out on warring expeditions when his wife is visited by a "noblelooking man," who tells her that she should bear him a son in order to save her husband's life. The next morning before leaving he spoke this verse:

I go home,

The pure pale morning draws near:
Manannán son of Lir
Is the name of him who came to thee.

Mongan was born from their union. It is also implied that Mongan is a rebirth of Finn mac Cumaill, "though he would not let it be told."

A fourth cycle involving the rebirth teaching is that of Finn mac Cumaill. Here we find the motif of the posthumous son who becomes a great hero. Cumaill is killed in battle, leaving his wife pregnant with his seventh son. When the boy is born, he is secretly fostered and nurtured in a remote forest area. Later, the king of Bantry, into whose service he anonymously enters, says: "If Cumaill had left a sone one would think that thou (Finn) wast he. However we have not heard of his leaving a son . . ." This motif is easily seen in the Mabinogi tale of "Peredur," and in its later development, *Parzival,* it is even more apparent. A Germanic parallel can be found in the saga of Sigurd.

So did the Celts hold the Pythagorean doctrine, or was it one of their own making? The Pythagorean school of metempsychosis is characterized by a sort of disdain for the physical vehicle, or body, which is said to be a prison for the soul. Pythagoreanism is also a highly moralistic philosophy. This moralistic foundation dictates that the soul be reborn into future circumstances determined by the degree of moral perfection attained in the previous existence.

For the Pythagorean school, it is also clear that a soul could transmigrate into any available human form being born at the time proper for the soul in question to be reincarnated. It is less clear whether or not Pythagoras taught that the human soul could be reborn in animal forms. The Celtic rebirth doctrine is not very moralistic—it is rather *vitalistic.* It is by sheer power and force of will and vitality that Gods, Goddesses and heroes gain rebirth. Also, it should be pointed out that the idea of being reborn in this world was thought to be a good thing—not an evil to be avoided.

Since there is plenty of evidence inside the Celtic tradition, and the Pythagorean system does not really explain that evidence very well, it seems more likely that the Celts were simply continuing with the age-old Indo-European rebirth ideas.

Especially strong in the Celtic tradition is the belief that the Tuatha Dé Dannan can engender children with mortal women—and that these heroes embody the basic qualities of the God in question. But this would be an exception rather than the rule in the normal course of human affairs.

More common is the regular rebirth of the dead ancestors in the bodies of their descendants. In this process, the soul (O.Ir. *enaid)* is reborn in the flesh of a newborn descendant. Between "incarnations," the soul is in the Underworld. There it awaits the right time and the right configuration of flesh to emerge from the Underworld to be reborn. While the soul is in the Underworld, however, it may make certain attachments and incur certain obligations—these will then perhaps be played out in this world.

Eventually, a soul may completely stop incarnating, or incarnations may become infrequent (as we measure time in this universe). It is only reluctantly that the soul will give up its existence in this world—despite the delights to be found in abodes such as the *Tír na mBan* or the *Tír na mBeo.*

Layout and Casting Methods

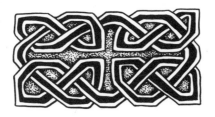

Chapter 5

Background

We are largely dependent on linguistic and comparative evidence for the reconstruction of the actual methods used by oghamic diviners. However, this evidence is rich, and our methods of analyzing this material are sophisticated enough that we can come to meaningful and useful conclusions as to exactly how these operations were carried out.

It is known, for example, that the oghamic characters were carved or notched onto four-sided elongated staves, called *crann-chur* in Old Irish and *coelbren* in Welsh, and that these were used in divinatory rites.

Furthermore, it is well known that all the Indo-European peoples had some sort of lot-casting as a form of divination—whether we are talking about the Teutonic folk with their runestaves or the Romans with their sortilege. As the Italic and Teutonic are the two peoples most related to the Celts among the Indo-European peoples, these are the best sources for any comparative evidence.

The most important things to establish in order to understand a folk, and hence their form of divination, is their cosmology and an analytical system that is a complete encoding of the natural order of the universe in some linear or quasilinguistic form. The cosmology gives a right-brain image of the world, and the analytical system provides a secret *metalanguage* of the world. In laying one over the other in a ritualized manner, reliable and consistent synchronicities can be produced which are harmonious with the worldview expressed by the systems involved. This is the way almost all systems of divination work: astrology (where the constellations in the heavens are juxtaposed to symbolic houses, and planets are juxtaposed to the constellations and houses, etc.), tarot (where cards are laid over certain reading positions), runes (where staves are cast onto steads of meaning) and so forth.

The ogham characters represent an analytical view of the world—this is true even if you take an almost profane view of ogham as purely a system of poetic diction and a method of memorizing things. It is after all a way to attempt to codify and classify all of existence in a meaningful way. Recent work has also fairly well established the true nature of the Celtic cosmological map, which provides the image into which these analytical characters can be "cast" in order to come up with divinatory readings. The recovery of these two keys was essential to the rediscovery of a true system of Celtic divination.

Working Methods

For a working of true divination to take place, the operator cannot enter into it with a profane or even mundane attitude. Working with the oghams is not a parlor game; it is a form of divination. When you divine, you are in the presence of the divine, and therefore the whole operation is to be approached with reverence and respect.

Figure 5.1: The Pattern of the Casting Cloth or Board

Making and Charging the Cloth

In divinatory operations, the oghamic fews are to be laid out or thrown upon a cloth or wooden surface. If cloth is used, it should be of a pure white color. If a wooden surface is used it should ideally be made of birch wood. The surface should be about three feet square and divided into sections, as shown in figure 5.1. If cloth is used, the bard can draw on it

with a permanent marker or ink, or the various lines and figures can be embroidered into the cloth. If wood or other hard
material is used, the patterns may be carved into the surface
and then painted. The colors may vary according to the taste
and wisdom of the bard—green or blue would in all circumstances be appropriate.

The actual construction of the cloth or board can be done in
a ritual setting—but at the very least the finished product should
be charged or blessed to the service of oghamic readings.

Lay the cloth or board before you and recite an invocation
to the forces of the directions:

Before me stands Eriu in Fal,
on my right stands Nuada in Gor,
on my left stands the Dagda in Mur,
and at my back stands Lugh in Fin.
May each bless me and go before me in all that I do here.

Or in a Christianized version:

Before me stands Master Morfessa of Falias,
on my right stands Master Esras of Gorias,
on my left stands Master Semias of Murias,
and at my back stands Master Uscias of Finias.
May each Master bless me and go before me in all that I do here.

Visualize four towering god-forms (or, in the Christianized
version, four old men) standing at the four cardinal points
directly to your left, right, before, and behind you. The one in
the north will be standing on a stone, the one to the right will
be holding a spear, the one to the left will be standing behind
a cauldron, and the one behind you will be holding a great
sword.

Then call the Gods and Goddesses to aid you in the blessing of your work:

I call upon all the Gods and Goddesses on which my forebears called and swore their oaths. Come, be with me in all I do here. I call upon the Dagda, the Good-God, upon Lugh the shining one, upon the strong Ogma, and upon Manannán of the Deep.

These god-forms might be varied in keeping with the personal needs and allegiances of the bard.

As a final blessing, either before beginning the work of creating the cloth or board or as a final act of blessing the completed form, speak the following words:

I call upon you, the three Brigids, to guide my hands and the ogham-fews. I call upon you, the three Morríghna, to guide my hand that I make the sign of the fifths good and true.

The casting cloth or board is a symbol of the macrocosmic world and as such is a highly sacred object and should be treated with great respect.

Making and Charging the Oghams

The actual pieces of wood, or fews, on which the ogham characters are carved can most easily be fashioned from quarter-inch-square pieces of wood. These can be found in most hobby or hardware stores. The fews can be almost any length, but the average useful length will probably be found to be three to four inches. The ogham is carved along one edge with the feather sign at the opposite end. An example diagram of the few for *straiph* is seen in figure 5.2. However, you can also just draw the characters on slips of cardboard and get similar results.

Ideally, the actual wood used for the construction of the fews would correspond to the name of the tree-ogham. For example, the birch-few would be made of birch wood, the rowan-few of rowan wood, and so forth.

To make the fews in a ritual manner, you should first cut 20 pieces of the wood (or other material) that you are using. Place them before you along with a knife or other carving device and red ink or paint (with a brush or other applicator). To your right hand should be an open flame (a candle will do) and to your left hand a container of open water.

First read the invocation to the forces of the directions:

Before me stands Eriu in Fal,
on my right stands Nuada in Gor,
on my left stands the Dagda in Mur,
and at my back stands Lugh in Fin.
May each bless me and go before me in all that I do here.

Or in a Christianized version:

Before me stands Master Morfessa of Falias,
on my right stands Master Esras of Gorias,
on my left stands Master Semias of Murias,
and at my back stands Master Uscias of Finias.
May each Master bless me and go before me in all that I do here.

Visualize four towering god-forms (or, in the Christianized version, four old men) standing at the four cardinal points directly to your left, right, before, and behind you. The one in the north will be standing on a stone, the one to the right will be holding a spear, the one to the left will be standing behind

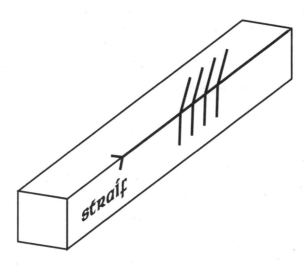

Figure 5.2: Example of the straif few

a cauldron, and the one behind you will be holding a great sword.

Then call the Gods and Goddesses to aid you in your work:

I call upon all the Gods and Goddesses on which my forebears called and swore their oaths. Come, be with me in all I do here. I call upon the Dagda, the Good-God, upon Lugh the shining one, upon the strong Ogma, and upon Manannán of the Deep.

These god-forms might be varied in keeping with the personal needs and allegiances of the bard.

Before beginning the actual carving of the fews, speak the following words:

I call upon you, the three Brigids, to guide my hands and the ogham-fews. I call upon you, the three Morríghna, to guide my hand that I make the fews good and true.

Carve the oghamic characters into each of the fews in turn. Begin with *beithe* and end with *idad*. After you finish carving the notches into the wood, color the notches, the feather sign and the edge between them with the red ink or paint. Set it aside to dry and take up the next few to be carved and colored.

To bless or charge the fews in order to dedicate them to true service, sprinkle each few with a bit of water from the container at your left hand and then pass it over the open flame to your right while silently thinking of the ogham name. You can also periodically do this operation with the water and flame to renew or "clear" the fews from any distracting influences which might collect around them over time.

Your fews should be stored in a cloth or leather bag large enough to hold the sticks very loosely. The bag is most appropriately green, blue or blue-green in color. In the case of a leather bag, it can, of course, be of a natural texture and color.

The Ritual of Reading the Oghams

Although the bard does not need to go into elaborate ritual each time an ogham reading is made, it may be wise to have some ritual to ensure that the process is respected. Those dedicated to elder Celtic paths, such as Druidiactos, would never want to dispense with a call to the ancestral Gods—Patrick's laws and dogmas no longer bind them.

Before beginning the reading, you should have a set place were the reading is to occur. Clear a space on a table or on your personal altar, or on the bare ground (covered with the casting cloth) on which the fews are to be laid or cast. If possible spread the cloth in front of you due north of your position as shown in figure 5.3.

North

Figure 5.3: Arrangement of the Casting-Cloth

One of the benefits of using the casting-cloth, even as a surface for your layout type readings, is that a sacred space is provided for the fews, and so complex geomantic arrangements become less necessary.

The rites of current oghamic divination are not necessarily complex, but they should be carried out with an appropriate level of formality. Before each working, the operator should (1) empower herself with a *lorica*-working, (2) invoke the Gods and Goddesses who give her power and insight, (3) call for the guidance of the Morríghna and/or Brigid in the operation, (4) do the actual layout or casting, (5) focus attention by means of a magical gesture (hands on the cheeks or over the eyes, thumbs or fingers put in mouth) and finally (6) make the reading or interpretation of the staves in an insightful and focused state of mind.

Although readers might perhaps do their own research and come up with ritual forms more suited to their own needs, here I have provided a traditional ritual formula making use of authentic Celtic heritage.

I. **Opening:** In order to sanctify and protect the place of working, a blessing of protection should be performed. Face north and hold your arms straight out to your sides in a cross-like posture and say:

Before me stands Eriu in Fal,
on my right stands Nuada in Gor,
on my left stands the Dagda in Mur,
and at my back stands Lugh in Fin.
May each bless me and go before me in all that I do here.

Or in a Christianized version:

Before me stands Master Morfessa of Falias,
on my right stands Master Esras of Gorias,
on my left stands Master Semias of Murias,
and at my back stands Master Uscias of Finias.
May each Master bless me and go before me in all that I do here.

While you are doing this, strongly visualize four towering god-forms (or, in the Christianized version, four men of ancient aspect) standing at the four cardinal points directly to your left, right, before, and behind you. The one in the north will be standing on a stone, the one to the right will be holding a spear, the one to the left will be standing behind a cauldron, and the one behind you will be holding a great sword.

II. **Invocation:** Still facing north, hold your arms out straight before you and say:

I call upon all the Gods and Goddesses on which my forebears
called and swore their oaths. Come, be with me in all I do here.
I call upon the Dagda, the Good-God, upon Lugh the shining
one, upon the strong Ogma, and upon Manannán of the Deep.

These god-forms can be varied according to the personal needs and allegiances of the bard.

III. **Call:** Now take up your position at the table, altar, or ground-space where you will actually cast or lay the fews. Hold your hands just below your mouth, palms upward, and say over them:

I call upon you, the three Brigids, to guide my hands and the
ogham-fews. I call upon you, the three Morríghna, to guide my
mind and the ogham-fews that I might see and read in them
what is right and true.

IV. **Layout or Casting:** Now proceed to cast the fews or lay them out on the cloth in the predetermined order as they are drawn one at a time from the bag. Once the fews are in their rightful places for the method you are using, you may go on to the ritual gesture.

V. **Gesture:** As a way to settle and concentrate your mind on the task at hand, you may want to use a ritualized gesture. Traditional versions of this might involve placing your palms over your eyes, or biting your thumb or finger to the point of causing significant pain. The former accentuates the withdrawal from the realm of the senses that some find beneficial to this kind of work, while the latter concentrates the whole self in the realm of the senses—awakening the self to the work before it.

VI. **Reading:** Once the fews have been laid or cast and your mind has been made ready to read them, you may begin to interpret the fews according to the kind of layout or casting chosen. Whether you are reading the oghams for yourself or another person, it is probably best to speak your thoughts about the reading out loud as you are making the interpretation. In the process of objectifying your thoughts—bringing them into the outside world—they will crystalize and take on more significance and be more intelligible.

Once the reading is complete, make a record of it and reverently and respectfully return the fews to their place of storage. A record of the readings is important because you will want to look for patterns developing in the readings over time and you may want to look back at readings you did as much as a month or a year before. Also, the fews may begin to "speak" a unique and personalized language with you—past readings will be found to be a great aid in decoding these personalized synchronicities.

Methods of Reading Oghams

Here I will present four methods of reading ogham-fews. It is perhaps best for you to try out all four in order to find out which one seems to work best for you at this time. Then specialize for a time in that method until you have mastered it—and made it fully a part of your whole outlook on the ogham and its interpretation. Then, if you feel it necessary, go on to try one of the other methods. Each has a special purpose, but each one can convey the same kind of essential information to your consciousness.

1. The Threefold Layout

The Way of Brigid

This is the simplest of the oghamic layouts. It is based on the cosmological tradition of there being three main realms or levels of existence: the upper world or Otherworld, this world *(bith)* and the lower world or Underworld, and on the tradition of the threefold aspects of certain Celtic Gods and Goddesses, such as Brigid and Lugh.

The threefold spiral, or triskelion, has often been identified as a particularly Celtic sign. Although this sign is found throughout the Indo-European world—among the Teutons and Greeks, for example—it does convey the particularly dynamic interplay of the three realms found in Celtic lore.

This threefold layout is a method of analyzing the nature of that interplay in your life at the present moment. The fews are

The Triskelion

to be chosen at random from your bag or from the bundle of fews in your hand and laid at a right angle to a vertical line from bottom to top in the order and manner shown in figure 5.4.

1. The bottommost few represents the Underworld aspect. It tells you what the root of the problem of question is. It may also refer to the organic basis of the question—things hidden in the dim, dark past—even from previous existences. It may also refer to matters of money, wealth or the erotic. From this root (in the past), the other aspects emerge.

2. The middle few tells you what the present situation is. It is the aspect of this world—or *Bith*. The information conveyed by this few may or may not be clear to you as you start the reading. This can be a clear illumination of the matter as it stands right now. It should always be read in the light of the first few. See how the Underworld few gives rise to the few of this world. The middle few also tells you about the state of your physical force or power at this time. It tells you what your manifest strength or weakness is.

3. At the top is the Otherworld aspect. It tells you what the

(3) [   ]

(2) [   ]

(1) [   ]

Figure 5.4: The Layout of Brigid

probable outcome of the situation should be, given the root and present situation. Of the three, this is the most fluid one. The Otherworld is not a steady-state. It is in a constant state of flux and is really a realm in which virtually all possibilities exist—a series of parallel universes, if you will. This few gives you some insight into the direction you are flowing. It is with this few that you are asked to use your gifts of will and intellect to become conscious of your direction and either alter it or go into it will a fuller awareness.

This method is perhaps the most subjective of the four presented here. It objectively shows less data to the reader, but the freedom or latitude in the various interpretations of the meanings of the fews is broadest here. This method will probably be favored by those with already highly developed psychic powers.

Sample Reading in the Way of Brigid

Question: *Should I resign from a spiritual organization with which I am presently involved?*

Note: The subject had been involved in two spiritual organizations for some time, and had assumed a leadership role in one of them, which was very demanding on his time.

The layout is done and the positions of the fews are recorded.

Records of layouts done by this method do not need to be any more complex than the diagram shown in figure 5.3. Simply inscribing the Roman letters for the three fews in the proper order does quite nicely. Under each letter, you can make a listing of the data relevant to the reading and maintain a permanent yet flexible record of the interpretation.

Reading: In the past, the subject has been in a state of flux and change (R), but old things and relationships have been fading, while new things and relationships have been becoming more vivid and important.

At present, the subject is in a phase in which he is concentrating his energies—a choice must be made. The central challenge of the moment is the courage to simplify life. There may also be a member of the opposite sex as a help-mate in this simplification.

The future will hold a steady foundation if purity and authenticity of effort is sought and found. However, the subject is warned that the future will not be without its struggles and conflicts. Steadfast loyalty to the foundation is the key to a successful outcome.

Final note: The subject did resign from the organization that was of secondary importance to him.

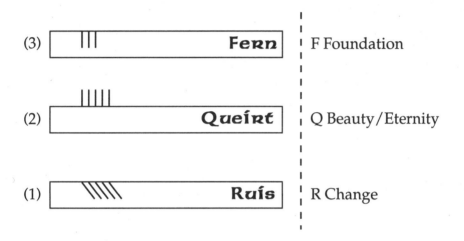

(3) | ┃┃┃ **Fern** ¦ F Foundation

(2) | ┃┃┃┃┃ **Queirt** ¦ Q Beauty/Eternity

(1) | ╲╲╲╲╲ **Ruís** ¦ R Change

Figure 5.5: Sample Reading in the Way of Brigid

2. The Fivefold Layout

The Way of the Fifths

The cosmological significance of the fivefold pattern of a center surrounded on four sides by fields or planes is already well known from the material presented in chapter 3. This five-fold pattern is certainly the best understood scheme of inner Celtic lore. Some might like to link this to the figure of the pentagram, although there is little evidence for the use of this figure before the Middle Ages. The most traditional pattern is simply the center surrounded in a cross-like figure on all four sides. The deep significance of this pattern to the ancient, pre-Christian Celts may explain to some extent the extreme popu-larity of the cross symbol in Celtic Christian lore.

When making use of this method, the bard should keep in mind all that he or she knows about how the "Fifths" work and what their significances are. (These are extensively discussed throughout this book.)

As the Way of Brigid was perhaps the most subjective of the four methods, the Way of the Fifths is perhaps the most objective. In this method strong use is made of the interpretations of the Fifths found in the tables of interpretation in chapter 6.

This fivefold layout is a method of analyzing the nature of the interplay of the forces present in the Fifths in your life at the present moment. You stand at the center of a cross-flow of forces, this reading helps you understand this confluence of powers. The fews are to be chosen at random from your bag or from the bundle of fews in your hand and laid out in the order and manner indicated by the numbers shown in figure 5.6.

The fews lying in these positions are to be read initially and most simply according to the tables presented for the Fifths in chapter 6. (See the example below for a practical guide to how this is done.) But beyond this there are subtle aspects that must be taken into account for the Way of the Fifths to find its full meaning.

This reading is ideal for learning of the state of a subject's being and the various influences which give rise to and condition that state. This is also true of the fourth method, but this one is suited not only to personal subjects, but also to impersonal ones—such as institutions, ideas or undertakings.

From the oghamic perspective, the cosmic Fifths are defined and symbolized by the *forfedha*. In turn, the Fifths help us understand the meanings of these mysterious symbols. Fews cast or laid in the Fifths, each of which is governed by a *forfidh*, are to be read and understood within the meaning of that symbol according to the following keys:

✕ (ea)—*Mide/Rige:* Indicates the ultimate focus and the beginning and ending of all understanding—the self. This is the reference point for all readings. This may some-

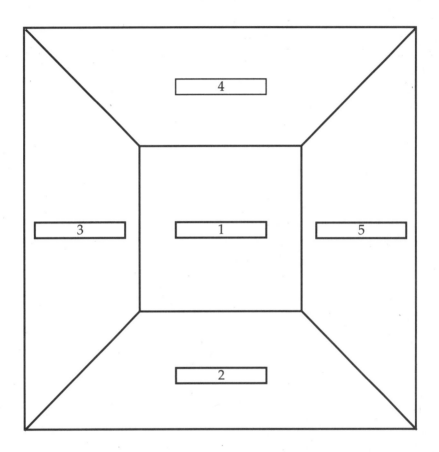

Figure 5.6: The Layout of the Fifths

times be a "collective self" when a reading is being done for a pair of lovers, a family, a group or an institution.

◇ (oi)—*Seis:* Indicates the space in which what has hap-
X   pened in the past has occurred. The few (or fews) in this field lies in past-space. This is the distant past.

⊘ (ui)—*Fis:* Tells what influences have been most recently
X developing—or "spiraling"—with regard to the question or subject. This is the recent past.

ᚎ (io)—*Cath*: Indicates things or influences which may provde resistance or conflict in the near future or in the present. If fews which are highly dynamic or personally empowering to the subject fall in this field, there is usually an indication of a lack of conflict or resistance here.

ᚏ (ae)—*Blath:* Tells what the final manifestation or out- come of the question will be given all the various crossing influences, which form a complex weaving together of inter- secting lines of force. This finally reflects on the subject of the reading and gives some indication of what the immediate future might hold.

In reading the layout, begin with the center in order to identify the state of the subject of the reading. After that, go around the four outer fields in numerical order to get a gen- eral understanding of the meanings conveyed by the oghams as they spiral around the subject. Then read positions 2 and 4 together—seeing how one flows to the other—and do the same for positions 3 and 5. Usually, the flow of influence is from position 2 to 4 and from 5 to 3. This is in keeping with tra- ditional flow patterns in the streams of power flowing in the earth. After both the spiraling order and the oscillating pat- terns have been looked at, perhaps a new understanding of the state of the central position of the subject will be reached. It is also possible to draw one more ogham-few to lay across the cen- tral position as a way of further elucidating its meaning.

Beyond the keys given above for meanings of the Fifths as governed by the *forfedha,* further keys to interpretation which help in forming a coherent interpretation of the fivefold lay- out are:

1. *Rige/Mide:* Kingship—the sovereign center. This is the over all state of being in which the subject is found.

2. *Seis:* Music/Harmony—the sword. This is the state of being influencing things in the subject's life having to do with harmonies; that is, those things with which the subject is perhaps interacting with on a harmonious or sympathetic level. This also shows the true basis of the whole question or problem being addressed in the reading. However, with certain fews, this may end up having negative—or disharmonious—reactions. This may have something to do with the emotional state of the subject.

3. *Fis:* Learning/Awareness—the cauldron. This is the state of being influencing things in the subject's life having to do with intellectual or spiritual aspects. These may be the aspects which one is aware of, or of which one should become aware. Here it is revealed what things the subject needs to learn. This position also has to do with the mental or spiritual state of the subject.

4. *Cath:* Battle/Conflict—the stone. This is the state of being influencing the inner and outer conflicts in the subject's life. These may be conflicts one must deal with, or they may be ways in which one will meet such conflicts in life. This position has much to do with the emotional state of the subject—especially if it is anger or fear.

5. *Blath:* Prosperity/Well-being—the spear. This is the state of being influencing things in the subject's life concerning matters of material well-being and health, as well as love life. It also indicates the full physical manifestation of the matter in question. This is the position of the "final outcome."

Sample Reading in the Way of the Fifths

Question: *What do my career plans look like? What is happening with me with regard to my plans for the future?*

The layout is done and the positions of the fews are recorded.

Records of layouts done by this method need not be any more complex than the diagram shown in figure 5.7. Simply inscribing the Roman letter for the few in the proper Fifth is quite sufficient.

Reading: The R in the first, middle, position indicates that the whole question is steeped in an issue of change. The secondary reading of Ruis in Mide (or "change" in "sovereignty") shows that there are essential changes going on in the subject's life— and that they perhaps hinge on the idea of maturity.

The basis of the whole, or the background of the issue, is one of inwardness or subjectivity, as indicated by the M *(muin)*. The subject of the reading has been harmoniously involved with his own subtle inner world in the past. This has been the area in which most of the subject's emotional life has been invested.

That which the subject must now learn is shown by the Z-few or *straiph* (control). The subject is being directed to learn about control, and also to realize the degree to which he has been controlled or coerced by circumstances outside his control in the past. This has been a period of testing.

The area which might be a source of future conflict is shown by the I-few (death/transformation). This indicates that there might be a significant fear (see Fifth reading for idad in cath) of the very transformations which make up the whole context of the reading situation.

In the last position, the A-few (objectivity sovereignty) shows that the outcome is one in which that which had been a matter of external control (Z) will become objective and self-governed (sovereign) control.

Finally, the whole reading shows that the subject's career

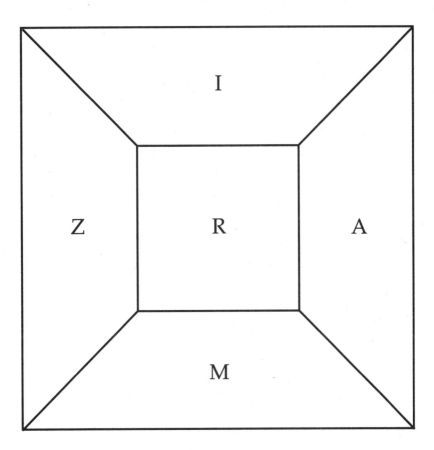

Figure 5.7: Sample Reading in the Way of the Fifths

plans are in a state of change and flux, with a foundation or basis in an inner world, which is being turned outward at this time. There is a certain inner conflict and fear about this change. But if the subject learns that the real issue is one of control—"Who's in control of the situation?"—then the final outcome will be one in which the subject will be able to exercise sovereign power.

3. The Fivefold Casting

The Way of Casting on the Fifths

The lore important to the understanding of the fivefold casting is identical to that of the cosmological lore discussed under the Way of the Fifths. The casting method allows for more random occurrence in what the bard is actually able to read in the lay of the fews in the planes of meaning.

Of all the kinds of oghamic readings, this is certainly the most complex and perhaps comprehensive. It combines a high degree of objective data with a good deal of subjective latitude for refined interpretation.

In procedure, this method differs from all the others. The bard will cast—actually throw—the fews onto the cloth at the point in the ritual where the fews are usually laid out. This should be done in a random fashion. Allow the fews to fall scattered over the cloth in whatever pattern they will. The resulting image is boundless in its possible varieties and thus allows for a very high level of interpretative sophistication. All 20 fews may be scattered out over all five (or nine) fields, or, theoretically, all 20 could fall into just one plane.

To begin with, read the fews in the same way, according to the same planes of meaning, as if they had been laid in those fields. In principle, this is an expanded version of the simple Way of the Fifths. It is just that there will usually be more than one few in each of the planes. It therefore becomes part of the work of the bard to synthesize the meanings of the multiple fews in each of the planes before coming to a general interpretation for that plane and how it affects the central subject.

Other important matters which must be taken into account include the number of fews in each of the planes, whether a few is lying across a boundary between planes, and even the line along which the few is lying or the direction in which it seems to be pointing. These matters give this kind of reading a vast amount of potential for subjective insight that can grow as the bard's level of understanding and ability with the system develop.

Although the fields of meaning are most traditionally held at the fivefold level, some readers may wish to combine the casting method with the ninefold pattern of fields seen in the fourth method discussed below. Again it is best to master one way of reading before going on to do serious work with another.

With the casting method, it is very important to make careful records of the readings. This must be done by actually drawing the fews on a diagram of the fields as shown in the sample casting below. This is because you may wish to review the casting at a later time, and no other way of recording it will preserve the subtleties and ambiguities of few alignment, borderline positionings and so forth.

Sample Reading in the Way of Casting on the Fifths

Question: *What will be the result or outcome of our corporation's move into a new location?*

The background of this question is that there was a group of people with a common cause who wanted to set up a separate meeting place where they could have meetings and hold seminars.

The casting is done, and the positions of the fews are carefully drawn and recorded as shown in figure 5.8. In making such a record, the bard must indicate the direction the line of the few makes, as shown, and carefully note where the few lies with regard to the lines of the diagram of the Fifths on the cloth.

In reading such a casting, the bard will begin with the middle and move in the same spiraling direction used in the Way of the Fifths or Way of the Worlds, and again an oscillation between the opposing fields or planes will be taken into account. The fact that more than one few can be in a Fifth, and that the fews can be crossing, touching or otherwise significantly juxtaposed to one another is the unique aspect of this method of oghamic reading. When clusters of fews occur, such as we have in this reading, special attention must be given to them also.

1. *Mide:* U and D are crossing—or opposing—each other. Inspiration and realization are coming to a head. The situation has to do with great principles (F in *mide*) and with dominion, and the question of harmony in this dominion. (Note that the L-few makes a bridge between the sovereign center and the southern realm of harmony.)

2. *Seis:* Note that there are no fews completely in the realm of harmony. Only the L-few bridging from the center and the N-few (REBIRTH) from prosperity. In the south, the N-few indicates *tyranny.*

3. *Fis:* Again note that there are remarkably few characters in the western Fifth concerning learning and awareness—only the Z-few (CONTROL), which in this Fifth can mean that there will be a certain amount of testing coming into the picture.

4. *Cath:* Here is the large cluster of the T-, Q-, S- and B-fews. In this field, almost all of these have decidedly negative connotations (vengeance, doubt, advantage, fury, and pride). Most telling, however, ia the H-few (MISFORTUNE), which crosses in the fields of three of the Fifths. The connotations of it in these three Fifths are weakness, defeat, and poverty. This cluster indicates that, as things stand right now, the whole project is in great trouble.

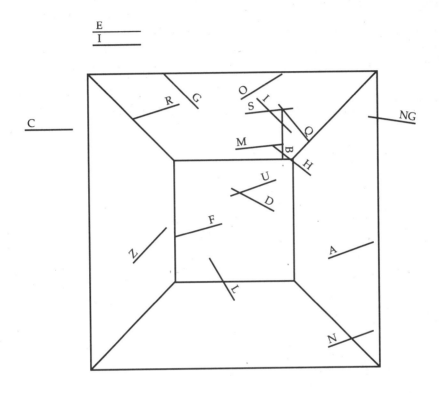

Figure 5.8: Sample Reading in the Way of Casting on the Fifths

(5) *Blath:* The H-few crosses into this Fifth—which directly connects the misfortunate cluster in the northern Fifth with the realm of Prosperity. The NG-few in this Fifth (good manners) is almost lacking—as it only barely touches the cloth. While the N-few in this Fifth indicates impoverishment (bridged from the southern Fifth, where it indicates tyranny).

When all of the elements in this reading are synthesized, it is clear that there will be a great deal of conflict and disharmony involved with this project, which will likely lead to a bad end. Those who are thinking about this project should be warned that certain steps should be taken to counteract these negative influences. There is a need for those elements which are lacking in the reading: namely those embodied in the C-, E-, and I-fews—or CREATIVITY, OVERCOMING and TRANS-FORMATION.

These kind of readings can, of course, be the most valuable type. In these insights, we can see what might potentially go wrong in a future situation and we are informed to some degree about what can be done to help remedy the negative circumstances—or help us to know what we must simply accept.

4. The Ninefold Method

The Way of the Worlds

In the methodology of the tarot, if there is anything really Celtic about the so-called "Celtic Cross" method, it lies in an expanded (really *unfolded)* view of the fivefold pattern of the Celtic Fifths. This is perhaps an example of suppressed "racial memory" unfolding in an unexpected area.

One of the main reasons for including this method is that it may provide a bridge between the methodology of the tarot and that of the oghams. The usual habit in the "Celtic Cross" layout in the tarot of lining the last four cards up in a row out to the right of the actual cross seems misguided from the traditional point of view. The last four "cards" (here ogham-fews) should really continue to encircle the central subject. Then a truer sense of the interrelationships of the cards or fews and how they interact with the subject can be seen.

Although this is really a method of laying the fews, they can also be cast upon this matrix using all the skills necessary to such a reading as discussed for the third method above.

The fews should be laid out in the order and pattern shown in figure 5.9.

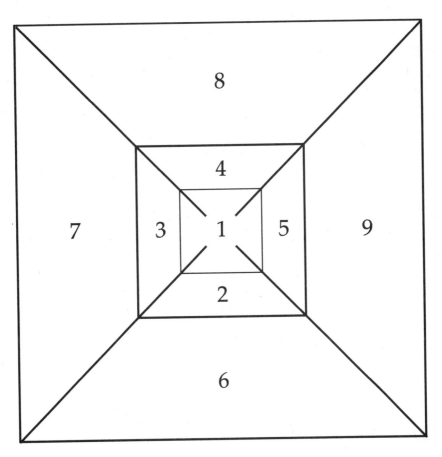

Figure 5.9: The Pattern of the Ninefold Layout

These positions are to be interpreted according to the following keys:

1. Indicates the present state of the self of the subject

2. Indicates the basis or background of the matter or problem in question as it relates to the subject—matters already a part of the subject's life experience

3. Indicates the influences just passing away in the life of the subject

4. Indicates that which might be an influence or state of mind toward which the subject is developing

5. Indicates an influence which will be in effect in the very near future for the subject

6. Indicates the fears of the subject, or the things which he or she may fear or be anxious about in the future

7. Indicates the familial and social environment in which the subject is found

8. Indicates the hopes and ideals of the subject

9. Indicates the final outcome of the whole situation and the place of the subject in it

In general, the inner ring or set of four planes (positions 2–3–4–5) have most to do with the inner or subjective states of the subject, while the outer ring (positions 6–7–8–9) have to do with the outer life and things affecting it.

Special attention should be given to the relationships of adjacent positions (2/6; 3/7; 4/8; 5/9) both to one another and to their combined effect on the subject. These pairs oscillate between each other and have a combined influence on the life of the subject. Again, there is both a spiral of power and meaning swirling around the subject and direct flows of force moving toward and across the subject.

The meanings of the fews as reflected in the various Fifths can also be taken into account (positions 2/6 in the south, positions 3/7 in the west, positions 4/8 in the north and positions 5/9 in the east).

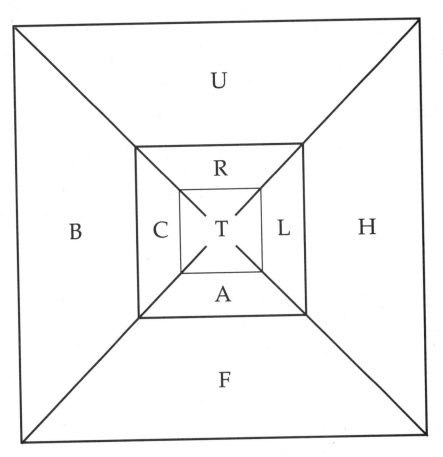

Figure 5.10: Sample Reading in the Ninefold Method

Sample Reading in the Ninefold Method

Question: *What will be the state of my relationship with my significant other this weekend?*

The layout is done and the positions of the fews are recorded as shown in figure 5.10. Records of layouts in this method do not need to be any more complex than the diagram shows. The simple inscription of the corresponding Roman letter for the few in the proper chamber is plenty.

Reading: Position 1 indicates that the present state of the self of the subject is essentially one of balance—in a state of self-possessed equilibrium. This gives the whole reading a good aspect and sets a hopeful tone.

Position 2 shows that the basis of the matter in question relates to the subject as one of sovereign independent person. This sovereign or independent and empowered state is already a part of the subject's life experience. This will continue to color the things happening in the relationship.

Position 3 indicates that a certain amount of creativity is just passing away in the life of the subject. There will be little more of a creative impetus in the relationship in the time frame posed.

In position 4, that which might be an influence or state of mind toward which the subject is developing is shown to be change. There is therefore some dynamism in the offing, but it will not be of a creative or original sort.

Position 5 indicates that there will be a great insight and quickening in the relationship in the time frame indicated.

In position 6, we see that there is an indication of the fears of the subject as being ones of stagnation and a fear of defeat or failure in the endeavor of making a better relationship with his lover. This fear of failure must be guarded against. When viewed together with position 2, this shows that the subject may be fearing something having to do with his perception of himself as an independent being.

Position 7 shows that the familial or social environment in which the subject and his lover are found is one full of vitality. That is, there will be a good number of unknown qualities in the time frame of the reading. The subject is advised not to be anxious about these but to embrace them for the vitality they provide. This few, together with that of the C-few in position 3, shows a virtual neutralization of these forces. The fact that creativity is passing away in the subjective realm and vitality is growing in the objective realm should be taken into account—but the subject should be forewarned that this may just lead to a sense of frustration, as the inner and outer worlds are not especially harmonious in the time frame in question.

In position 8, the hopes of the subject are revealed to be ones involving a gateway to new beginnings and new levels of renewed passion in life and in the relationship. The hope is for a gateway to renewal. Contrary to the mixed signals sent by the combination of the fews in positions 3 and 7, the R- and U-fews in positions 4 and 8 are quite harmonious and supportive of one another. Both indicate an opening to new things. This combination should be kept in mind as the subject tries to hold onto an objective appreciation of his situation in life.

Position 9 is a significant sign that there may be trouble in the whole reading. It indicates misfortune. It may be a warning of possible misfortune, or it may be a sign of the destruction of old and detrimental things. The overall governance of the reading by the T-few in the middle might be an indication of the positive interpretation. Or it may simply be showing that the high hopes of indicated by position 6 will simply not be realized in the time frame. Reading positions 9 and 5 together, we see that any misfortune can be tempered by insight and quickening. The knowledge provided by the oghamic reading may, in this case, prove to be transformative when conveyed to the subject.

Note: In retrospect, the subject reported back that the reading was quite accurate. The whole weekend was one full of interactions with many kinds of people and the atmosphere of the time was very dynamic and rather light-hearted. However, the whole was very far from what he expected or really hoped for, in that on an intimate level of interaction with his lover was unfortunately lacking.

These methods and sample readings should give the potential bard some solid idea of how to go about performing oghamic readings in ways that can lead to great personal insights so that eventually the ogham fews can become powerful tools for self-counselling.

Alternate Ways of Drawing Fews

In all the methods outlined above, the bard is limited to reading each oghamic character only once in every reading. However, this may not produce the most accurate reading; it is quite possible that, in reality, a few could be manifest in more than one place in the situation.

Here are two more ways of drawing fews. When using the first method, you draw a lot from your bag and, depending on which layout pattern you are working with, trace that oghamic character on a piece of paper or in the loose earth or sand. Put the few back in the bag again and shake it, saying aloud or silently: "Morríghna guide my hand!" Then draw another few form the bag and note its proper place in the reading. Continue this process until you have completed the pattern of the chosen reading. Theoretically, you could end up with a reading that contains only one few repeated several times! This would be an unmistakable message.

The second method involves the use of an archaic form of "dice." In order to use this technique, the bard must make seven sticks or slips of wood that are broad and flat enough that if thrown onto a flat surface, they can only land with one

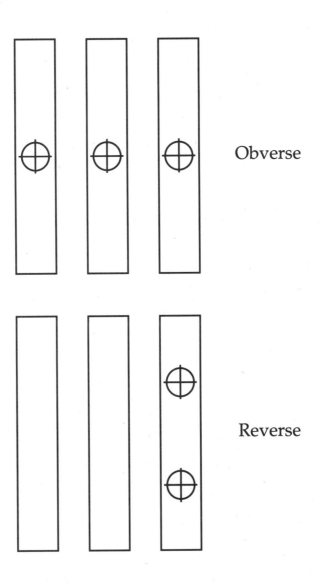

Figure 5.11: The *aicme*-sticks

side face up. Three of these sticks, the *aicme*-sticks, will be marked with a single sign (for example, with a four-spoked wheel) on one side, one side will be blank on the reverse of two of these sticks and the other will be marked with two signs on the reverse, as shown in figure 5.11. If these three sticks are thrown, they will naturally result in a number of 1, 2, 3 or 4. These will give the *aicme*-count of a particular oghamic few.

A second set of four sticks, the few-sticks, is to be prepared with another kind of marking (for example, a circle or point). All four of these have only one mark on one side, three of them are blank on the other side while the remaining one has two marks on it, as shown in figure 5.12.

Any throwing of these sticks will result is a number between one and five. These determine the particular few or oghamic character within the already determined *aicme* or family.

First you throw the *aicme*-sticks to get a number from one to three; then you throw the few-sticks to get a number between one and five. The resulting combination (for example, 3:3) identifies a particular few in the oghamic order—in this case, NG *(ngetal)*, the third few in the third *aicme*.

As each few in generated in this manner, note it in its proper place in the reading you are doing. The same few can occur several times in the same reading. This method allows for maximal freedom for the fews in layouts. Similar systems could be generated for the tarot.

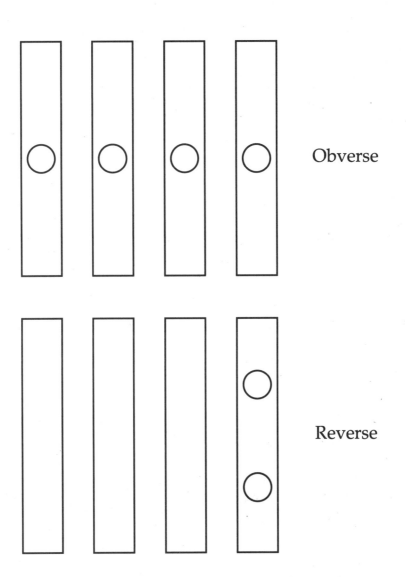

Obverse

Reverse

Figure 5.12: The few-sticks.

BIRCH

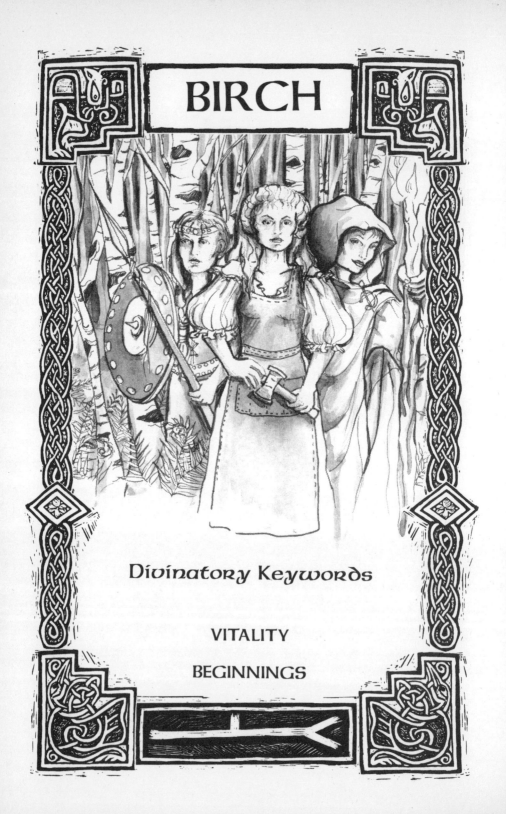

Divinatory Keywords

VITALITY

BEGINNINGS

Beithe  Birch

(Betula alba)

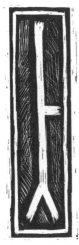 The birch is a tree known for its beauty and splendor in early spring, when its white bark shines through its splendid green leaves. The image of white shining through the green is an archetypal vision of the Otherworld. (Even in medieval romances with Celtic origins, when a woman is seen in a green dress with her white skin shining through slits in it—or in more modest and Christianized versions, with a white undergarment—it is a sure sign that the woman is "of the Otherworld.") It is said that the birch can protect a woman from being carried off to the *sídhe* or Otherworld.

Deities and Heroes

Brigid, daughter of the Dagda, is the Goddess most closely associated with the birch. She appears in three distinct roles or aspects which correspond to the poet (or magician), the warrior and the mother. Her cult was later Christianized under the guise of that of St. Brigid.

Another divine or semidivine figure related to the B is **Bran.** He is known as the divine navigator who sailed into the Otherworld. A mythic account of this voyage can be read in "The Voyage of Bran" (Cross and Slover, *Ancient Irish Tales,* 1936).

In the heroic mythology, *beithe* corresponds to **Bricriu,** who is called the "poison-tongue" (O.Ir. *Nemthenga)* because he incites heroes to rivalry and mutual contention—thus leading to their development and growth. (See "Bricriu's Feast" in *Ancient Irish Tales.)*

Diuinatory Meanings

The B has to do with new beginnings, the inception or birth of things and people. The energizing and vitalizing effect of this power provides for the protective aspect of the birch. It has the power to "drive out" evil or corrupting influences by means of its eternally vital life-force. (This is the original reason why birch was first used as an instrument in flagellant fertility rites and then later in judicial and recreational floggings in Europe and elsewhere.)

Birch, as the first of the oghamic trees, was also the preferred wood to be used in making oghamic staves for divinatory or magical purposes.

The birch tells you to realize the new and good by shearing away the old and detrimental. There is great strength and resilience deep within you. There may be choices to make. The birch is a very "lucky tree," and so is a sign of general good fortune.

However, the challenge of the birch is the need to deal with constant change and loss of familiar things as time goes on. You must learn to trust and to lose this fear of the unknown.

Professions

The B is the sign of the common, everyday work that many folk must do to make a living. The birch may also represent a common laborer or worker in a divinatory reading.

These, like most other professions in these interpretations, are largely drawn from a section in the *Scholar's Primer (Auraicept na N'Eces)* which makes such correspondences between oghams and professions. In that text, of course, professions whose Irish names begin with the sounds of the oghams correspond to those oghams. Let intuition be your guide in finding possible other links between professions or other human activities and the *fedha*.

The Fifths

Beithe in Mide	Vitality in Sovereignty	MEAD (+)
Beithe in Seis	Vitality in Harmony	DISTURBANCE (−)
Beithe in Fis	Vitality in Learning	EAGERNESS (+)
Beithe in Cath	Vitality in Conflict	FURY (+)
Beithe in Blath	Vitality in Prosperity	RICHES (+)

ROWAN

Divinatory Keywords

INSIGHT

QUICKENING

Luís  Rowan (or Quicken)

(Pyrus or Sorbus aucuparia)

The rowan or quicken tree has a powerful reputation in the sciences of magic and divination. It may also be known by the names quickbeam or mountain ash. Some of its reputation may come from the symbolic quality of its bright red berries.

"Quickbeam" means "living wood" in archaic modern English. Its berries are one of the "foods of the gods." Rowan wood is widely used as a magical substance for protection from lightning and from malevolent enchantments. Before a battle Druids of old are said to have kindled fires of rowan wood and spoken incantations over them in order to invite the inhabitants of the *sidhe* to take part in the fight.

Deities and Heroes

Lugh Lamfadha is the God corresponding to *luis*. He is the trifunctional or three-aspected high-God of the ancient Celts. In

this he is a reflection of the nature of Brigid (B). Lugh is the many-skilled (Irish *samildanach*) magician/king of the Gods, as well as a chief warrior (as the God of the spear), and he is also responsible for bringing the harvest—which expresses his agricultural side. In many ways, Lugh corresponds to the Teutonic God Wóden or Ódhinn.

Among the Goddesses, the *luis* corresponds to the **Leanan Sídhe,** an Otherworldly female figure who inspires poets and musicians, while in the heroic mythology the L is linked to **Loegaire,** the charioteer of CúChulainn, who at one point travels to the Mag Mell to rescue its queen.

Divinatory Meanings

Because the rowan gives special insight or foreknowledge, it can be seen as a tree of protection against enchantments. It provides forewarnings against such "enchantments," which may be most practically conceived of as any influence having its origins outside ourselves and of which we are not aware.

In divination the L indicates that you are to look within and seek for the insight necessary to overcome your problems. It portends that the inner vitality necessary to this insight is available, if you know how and where to look. The *luis* describes a vast sea of flooding vitality waiting to be tapped. Take heart, as any destruction you encounter will only be temporary.

The challenge of the rowan is the avoidance of being overly influenced by forces outside yourself. You may encounter inner feelings of doubt, and you may tend to be overextending yourself.

Professions

Luis may be the sign of a person who drives or steers a vehicle (especially on the waters). Nowadays this may include managers who guide the ship of the institution they manage. It may also indicate a person of this description in a divinatory reading.

Managers of this kind partake of both the sovereign aspect of leadership and the productive aspect bound up with the purpose of the institution or company they manage.

The Fifths

Luis in Mide	Insight in Sovereignty	DOMINION (+)
Luis in Seis	Insight in Harmony	CRAFT (+)
Luis in Fis	Insight in Learning	DISCOVERY (+)
Luis in Cath	Insight in Conflict	CUNNING (+)
Luis in Blath	Insight in Prosperity	ABUNDANCE (+)

ALDER

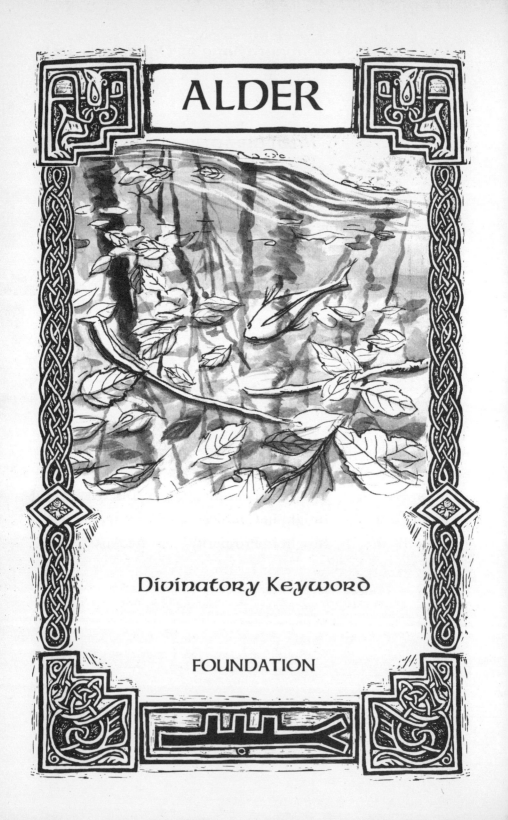

Divinatory Keyword

FOUNDATION

Fern  Alder

(Alnus glutinosa)

 Alder is a wood which resists the decaying or corrupting effects of water. Beams of alder were used in the underwater beam-construction of the ancient Celtic lake dwellings in present-day Switzerland (La Tene). It is thought that the tree contains a fiery energy, and it is for this mysterious reason that it is able to withstand water so well.

The alder is the tree of the divine hero Bran. The tree has the curious property of having white wood, at least when it is first cut, from which a red sap runs. This makes it appear to be a wounded man. From this tree both green and red dye are made: the green from its flowers, the red from its bark. Green is the color most associated with the "Otherworld" in Celtic lore. Wearing this color honors the inhabitants of the *sidhe*. The red corresponds to the fiery energy of the alder.

Deities and Heroes

In the divine mythology, the God corresponding to *fern* is **Fintan,** who survived the primeval flood and lived underwater in a variety of shapes (especially that of a salmon). He is the eternal repository and timeless foundation of wisdom and knowledge.

Among the Goddesses, the F refers to **Fotla,** one of the forms of the sovereignty of Ireland. In the heroic mythology, this sound corresponds to the great hero **Fionn mac Cumhail,** who is the foremost leader of the warrior-band *(fianna)* in Ireland. He gained magical knowledge when he stuck his thumb in his mouth to cool it after it had been burned on the salmon of knowledge (see Fintan!), which he was roasting. (There is an analogous Teutonic myth concerning how Sigurd gained "second sight" while roasting the heart of the serpent, Fafnir.) Fionn mac Cumhail is the subject of an entire heroic cycle. (See *Ancient Irish Tales.*)

Divinatory Meanings

Fern is a great strength in any contentious situation and is powerful in any competition. The alder is tenacious and determined in its power. The F indicates the very founding principles of all tradition.

As an oracle, the F indicates that you remain steadfast in what you know to be your true principles—the foundation of your knowledge and being. If you are unsure of what these founding principles are, the alder indicates that you should seek them relentlessly until they are found. You may, however, be found to be overresistant to change, if the alder is indicated in a place where you might be expecting movement and dynamism.

The challenge of the alder is not being aware of danger and dispute, and to have the knowledge of when to remain steadfast and when to allow and encourage change in life. You may have a tendency to fear defeat to such an extent that your courage is impaired.

Professions

Fern may indicate someone who is a poet or magician. But it may also indicate those interested in history or science of any kind.

The Fifths

Fern in Mide	Foundation in Sovereignty	PRINCIPLES (+)
Fern in Seis	Foundation in Harmony	QUICKNESS (+)
Fern in Fis	Foundation in Learning	LAZINESS (+)
Fern in Cath	Foundation in Conflict	VIGILANCE (+)
Fern in Blath	Foundation in Prosperity	OBSTRUCTION (−)

WILLOW

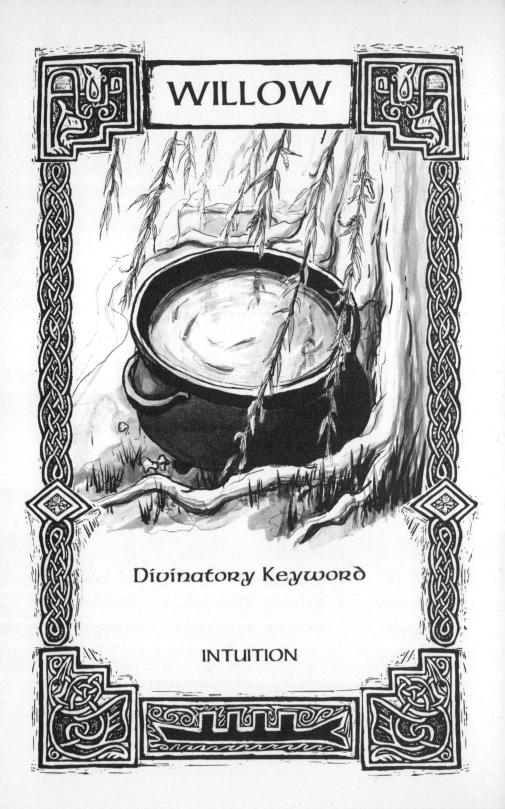

Divinatory Keyword

INTUITION

Sail  Willow

(Salix alba)

The willow is a tree fond of watery places. Because of this, it is sometimes associated with the moon and with divine figures who correspond to the moon. Branches of willow are often used as divining rods—especially for "water witching." From the Irish word, it can also be known as the "sally tree" in English.

The traditional witch's broom is made of three woods: birch, willow and ash: birch twigs for the broom itself, willow to bind them together and to hold them to an ash stake.

Willow has several medicinal uses as well. In ancient times salicylic acid drawn from its bark was used to relieve rheumatic pains—then thought to have been caused by malevolent magic.

Deíties and Heroes

In the divine mythology, the S corresponds to the God **Semias,** who is the master of wisdom and the original keeper

of the cauldron of knowledge in the Otherworldly city of Murias in the west. He gives this cauldron to the Dagda. Among the Goddesses, this sound is linked to the Goddess of Skye, **Scathach,** who is the teacher of CúChulainn. She teaches him skills in arms and foretells his future. In the heroic mythology, the S corresponds to **Setanta,** the boy-hood—pre-initiate—name of CúChulainn.

Divinatory Meanings

The willow is a sign of intuition, imagination and some-times even of deception. It is the unfoldment of psychic or clairvoyant powers. In the willow is a gift of cunning—of the skillful and subtle use of mental powers to have your aims met.

In divination, the *sail* indicates that there may be unfore-seen dangers for you or those you love. You have something to learn from an unseen or as yet unknown person (probably a woman). This lesson may be unpleasant, but it will be of great benefit. You are urged to seek out the hidden forces in your life.

The main challenge of the willow is the tendency to ignore the unconscious, the hidden aspects of the personality or the anima. You may be ignorant of an important aspect of your-self—which remains hidden.

Professions

The S can represent people involved in handicraft; that is, in any trade or work in which the hands are used in a skillful way to create or shape something. It may express the need for such skills. As with other "professions" in these interpretative sections, this may indicate that the skills are what need to be obtained in order to improve one's outlook for success.

The Fifths

Sail in Mide	Intuition in Sovereignty	INSIGHT (+)
Sail in Seis	Intuition in Harmony	SUBTLETY (+)
Sail in Fis	Intuition in Learning	CUNNING (+)
Sail in Cath	Intuition in Conflict	ADVANTAGE (+)
Sail in Blath	Intuition in Prosperity	LOATHING (−)

ASH

Divinatory Keywords

REBIRTH

PEACE

Nín   Ash

(Fraxinus excelsior)

The ash is a very magical tree. It has been used in the formulations of many medicines. The ash is a tree of some cosmological importance because of the symbolism of its curious compound leaf-formation: two or four pairs of leaves tipped by a single leaf, so the large compound leaf contains either five or nine total leaflets.

This tree's wood was also most often used in the construction of spears in ancient times.

Deities and Heroes

In the divine lore of the Irish, the N is expressed through **Nuada Airgetlam** (Silver Arm), who is the king of the Tuatha Dé Danann. He loses his hand in battle and thus is unable to continue to rule as king. Here we are reminded of the Norse God Tyr and his loss of a hand to the Fenris-Wolf. The Irish believed the king had to be of unblemished body in order to rule. He first had a silver hand made to replace his own, but

later one of actual flesh was grafted on. Nuada has Lugh rule while he is unable to do so. He is finally killed in the battle of Mag Tured. This God is the same as the more common Celtic Nodens, who is apparently a God of the waters.

Among the Goddesses, the N corresponds to **Niamh,** who is the daughter of the Sea God Manannán. She lures the hero Oisin into *Tír na n'Óg*—Land of Youth—where they spend 300 years. The N corresponds to the great royal hero **Niall,** who became king over Ireland after passing a test in which he was able to obtain water from a divine hag—by not only kissing her, but by lying with her also. The hag—or Caillach—is then revealed to be in truth the Goddess Eriu, the Goddess of the Sovereignty of Ireland.

Divinatory Meanings

The N-few is the link between the inner and outer worlds. The fivefold pattern (also reflected in nine) of the cosmos. From this map, we derive our link with cosmological wisdom. It makes us able to function in deep, "watery" places—in the realms of the Underworlds. It is our flexible psychic strength. It is the weave of fate and the guardian of peace.

Take care to see things in their larger context. Note how all actions have their reactions in the world, and note how you affect the world through your actions—both physical and spiritual. However, seeing these things—act. Take bold actions when action is called for.

The challenge of the N is the determination of hidden influences and appearances. Things are not always what they seem—and you, like Niall, must be perceptive enough to discern that which is noble. There is a tendency to spilt off from the environment, toward social or psychological insularity—to be cut off from the outside world.

Professions

True to the precision and hard-working aspects of the ash, the occupation that might be indicated by the N is that of notary or accountant.

The Fifths

Nin in Mide	Rebirth in Sovereignty	RENEWAL (+)
Nin in Seis	Rebirth in Harmony	TYRANNY (−)
Nin in Fis	Rebirth in Learning	SATISFACTION (+)
Nin in Cath	Rebirth in Conflict	AFFLUENCE (+)
Nin in Blath	Rebirth in Prosperity	IMPOVERISHMENT (−)

WHITETHORN

Divinatory Keyword

MISFORTUNE

Huath  Whitethorn (OR Hawthorn)

(Crataegus oxyacantha)

 In British folklore, the hawthorn is generally said to be a "bad luck sign." The destruction of a hawthorn bush will bring about great disaster for the one responsible. In Ireland, the hawthorn often grows around or over wells (as does the hazel bush), and these are the object of certain cultic rites involving the tearing of one's clothing and hanging the shreds on the hawthorn. This usually takes place toward the beginning of the month of May—a month ruled by the hawthorn.

The hawthorn has a dual sexual significance. It is both a sign of abstinence or asceticism, as well as of sexual abandon. The English go out on May Morning to pick hawthorn flowers before dancing around the Maypole. Sacred hawthorns appears to have been found all over the British Isles in ancient times. One grew in the confines of Glastonbury Abby, called the Glastonbury Thorn, which was cut down by the Puritans—no doubt due to its pagan associations.

Deities and Heroes

The H-few never occurs at the head of an Irish word, so there can be no divinities or heroes expressed by it. This very fact also point to its ominous and malevolent characteristics.

There is often an outer form connected with this few which is sensational, beautiful and seductive—but which is underneath destructive and detrimental.

Divinatory Meanings

The H-few councils cleansing: a need for the removal of that which weakens you. It councils the need for self-denial and self-sacrifice, which will lead to a general improvement in life. It warns, however, of a streak of bad luck or missed fortunes. The H-few councils restraint—keeping yourself to yourself. This is a stage of mental activity as a prelude to manifestation. Along with this, there may come a period of isolation, but in this loneliness will come the strength needed to overcome any misfortune—if all this is truly understood. There will be some disruption in the normal flow of life. Hopes will not be realized.

One of the many challenges of the H-few is the tendency to rush ahead too quickly. There is a need for gestation and patience. There is enforced inactivity, which will give rise to new opportunities. There may be cunning and voracious forces lurking beyond your knowledge. Another major challenge is the fear of success. You may secretly be sabotaging your own efforts due to a lack of self esteem and sense of self-worth.

Professions

This few corresponds to the composer of trisyllabic poetry, and so it may refer to a poet or the art of poetry. Because of the mysterious associations with this few, the type of poetry or creativity indicated may be of a rather dark type.

The Fifths

Huath in Mide	Misfortune in Sovereignty	WEAKNESS (−)
Huath in Seis	Misfortune in Harmony	DISHARMONY (−)
Huath in Fis	Misfortune in Learning	IGNORANCE (−)
Huath in Cath	Misfortune in Conflict	DEFEAT (−)
Huath in Blath	Misfortune in Prosperity	POVERTY (−)

OAK

Divinatory Keyword

ENDURANCE

Duír  Oak

(Quercus robor)

 There is perhaps no tree more storied in Celtic lore than the oak. Although it is true that the oak is not the supreme tree of Celtic lore as it was once thought to be, it is nevertheless of great importance. The acorns of the oak were typically used to feed swine—which are the Otherworldly or Underworldly animals par excellence. It was even thought that the bard or Druid could gain special inspiration by eating acorns. Oak groves were probably the typical site for many nemetons throughout the Celtic world from Britain to Galatia in Asia Minor. The environs of an oak are especially auspicious for workings of magic or divination. The oak is also often used as a natural marker for boundaries between geographical territories.

Its very name has to do with hardness and steadfastness, as it is derived from the Indo-European root *deru-*, to be firm, steadfast. It is the root which gives us not only "tree" in English, but also "truth" and "troth." One etymology of the word "Druid" derives it from *dru-wid-*, "knower of oak-trees"—although it could just as easily mean "knower of the

truth or troth"; i.e., "steadfast knowledge."

The oak, like the yew, can reach a great age and an enormous size. One of the largest ever reported is the Courthorp Oak in Yorkshire at more than 70 feet in circumference. The mythic Arthur's Round Table at Winchester is cut from a single slice of an oak tree.

Deities and Heroes

In Irish mythology, it is the **Dagda,** the "Good God," who corresponds to the D-few. The Dagda is the Celtic Zeus or Tyr. He carries a club as his weapon. The Dagda was probably originally the High God of the Irish. One of his alternate names is Eochu Ollathir—Eochu (= horse) the All-Father. His harp was called "the Oak of Two Greens" and the "four angled music." With this harp, the Good God was able to play three kinds of magical music: the laugh-strain, the sorrow-strain and the sleep-strain. The Dagda has a cauldron—brought from Murias—which receives the Druidic sacrifices and which forever dispenses endless blessings. He is the father of Brigid, the patroness of poets. For this and other reasons, the Dagda is considered the main God of the Druids. This association with the Druids indicates the extremely archaic nature of the Druidic cult and its linkage with the oldest established institutions in the Celtic culture.

Among the Goddesses of the Irish, it is **Danu** to whom the D-few belongs. She is the most remote and ancient ancestress of the Gods—who are called the Tuatha Dé Danann (the people of the Goddess Danu).

In the heroic mythology of Ireland, two figures may be strongly linked to the D-few—both of them examples of the tragedy of human endurance in the face of overwhelming odds. Among the female heroes of Ireland, **Deirdriu** or **Deirdre** is one of the most tragic. Cathbad, chief Druid of Conchobar, prophesied that she would bring destruction to Ulster. Therefore, the men of Ulster wanted her killed. However, she was secretly fostered to save her life. Eventually she was pursued by many chieftains, and the wars and conflicts over her indeed brought the greatness of Ulster into decline. She finally killed herself to avoid further shame. Her story is much like that of Helen of Troy.

Another tragic figure is found in **Diarmuid,** who was the nephew of Fionn and a hero within the Fianna. He was fostered in the Underworld and had a "love-spot" that made him irresistible to women. At one point, the aged Fionn goes with the Fianna to woo a young beauty named Grainne, but she falls in love with the youthful Diarmuid, and they run away together. Fionn lays a geis (magical restriction) that they cannot spend more than one night in one place. Eventually Fionn makes peace with Diarmuid, but later sends him to hunt a boar that he was supposed to avoid. Diarmuid is wounded by the boar, and Fionn refuses to give him a healing drink—as his jealousy raises to the surface again. There are many parallels between this tale and the Arthurian tale of Tristan and Isolda.

Divinatory Meanings

Duir is a sign of strength and endurance. It is the power needed to overcome all tests—even if the tests prove too great, the power of the oak will make a hero of the one who knows it. The oak is a symbol of fate and fatalism—as reflected in the tales of both Dairmuid and Deirdre. The D-few is a gateway to inner realms, a sign that reveals the truth about the past layers of action. This revelation gives strength and vision to the person who would try to see beyond the horizons of time both into the dim past and into the far future. In fact, the oak, as a sign for the balanced, empowers synthesis of all opposites.

In the oracular sense, the D-few advises that strength and endurance are yours in the situation. You should look to that strength to gain vision in order to overcome all obstacles. A gateway to new understanding is opening if you will be strong and true. There may also be some indication of your role as a leader of a group or fulfilling an executive position.

The challenge of the oak is the need to take up the charge of leadership. It may be a difficult task. Also there is a need for protection, a need to shelter yourself so that strengthening can take place. You may be pursued by unwanted and undesirable persons or forces—but strength and endurance must be drawn from the oak.

Professions

The occupation corresponding to the D-few is "Druidry"; that is, wizardry. This is therefore the sign of the magician, but it is also the sign of the worker in wood—the carpenter. It must also be pointed out that the essential meaning of the D-few indicates that those closely associated with it are steadfast and loyal in their dealings with others.

The Fifths

Duir in Mide	Endurance in Sovereignty	REALIZATION (+)
Duir in Seis	Endurance in Harmony	DISCONTENT (−)
Duir in Fis	Endurance in Learning	RECOGNITION (+)
Duir in Cath	Endurance in Conflict	DESTRUCTION (+)
Duir in Blath	Endurance in Prosperity	REST (+)

HOLLY

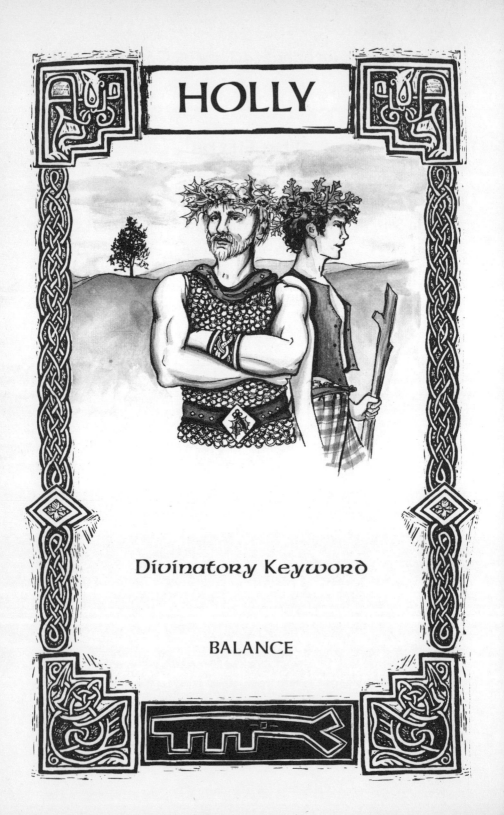

Divinatory Keyword

BALANCE

Tínne  Holly

(Ilex aquifolium)

 The holly is deeply steeped in lore on the British Isles. Holly was often used for the construction of chariot shafts. The chariot was the chief vehicle of the ancient Celtic warrior. The "Green Knight" (in the epic poem *Sir Gawain and the Green Knight*) is said to have a club made of holly wood. In the lore, the holly and the oak form a sort of twin pair. This may indeed have its roots in oghamic lore in that it may be linguistically based. The T- and D-sounds are really variants of one another. The only difference between the two is that, when one makes the D-sound, one's vocal cords vibrate and, when making the T-sound, they do not. This is the kind of lore important to poets and bards and other practitioners of verbal magic. (In the oghamic system, this same kind of lore can be noticed in the relationship between the C-sound and the G-sound.)

Deities and Heroes

In ancient Irish theology, the T-few can be ascribed to the great primordial being **Trefuilngid Tre-Eochair,** who, in the tale called "The Settling of the Manor of Tara," came to the men of Ireland and told them how to apportion the land according to the fivefold cosmological structure. This being is himself twofold and threefold (bearing in his left hand stone tablets and in his right hand a branch bearing three fruits—nuts, apples and acorns). This being is described as the force controlling the rising and setting of the sun (right natural order) and the repository of all history.

Among the heroes of Ireland, the T-few best expresses the essence of **Tigernmas,** a cultural hero who is said to have introduced the cult of Cromm Cruach, who some identify as Balor. Tigernmas also introduced the crafts of metallurgy and the weaving of tartans as clan insignia.

Divinatory Meanings

Tinne is a sign of revenge or vengeance taken for wrongs done to someone or to one's kith and kin. As a sign of perfect balance, it is that force which will act in retribution for wrongs done. The holly is a sign of justice and retribution.

For oracular readings, the T-few indicates a directed balance and a capacity to unify two sides of a question or problem. You are to be, as the holly is, steadfast in adversity—remaining green and vital during the coldness of winter. Even in adversity, your strength will increase. There may be some legal or money matters in the offing.

The challenge of the holly is that there is a lack of direction or balance, and that you might be at present unequipped to deal with present hardships or challenges. There is a need for more knowledge, perhaps, but certainly the need to communicate your ideas well and effectively.

Professions

In the traditional applications of professions to the oghams, we find that the T-few is ascribed to a "turner"; that is, a person who makes wheels and axles for chariots. This could also be applied to mechanics or engineers of all kinds today. In divination, it could signify a person of this trade, or simply stand for this kind of skill.

The Fifths

Tinne in Mide	Balance in Sovereignty	STEADFASTNESS (+)
Tinne in Seis	Balance in Harmony	REJECTION (−)
Tinne in Fis	Balance in Learning	JUDGMENT (+)
Tinne in Cath	Balance in Conflict	VENGEANCE (+)
Tinne in Blath	Balance in Prosperity	PREPARATION (+)

HAZEL

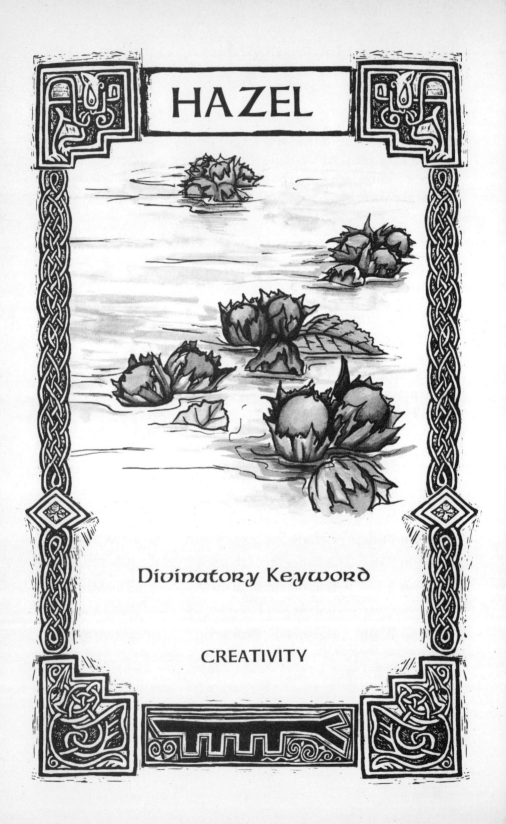

Divinatory Keyword

CREATIVITY

Coll  Hazel

(Corylus avellana)

The hazel is one of the most storied plants in Celtic lore. The most profound myth regarding it is found in the Irish tale called "Cormac's Adventures in the Land of Promise" *(Ancient Irish Tales,* 503-507). There it is recounted how Cormac went to the Otherworld to try to recover his wife, son and daughter, who had been abducted by Manannán mac Lir. While there, he saw a spring with nine hazels growing over it. The nuts of the nine hazels fall into the water. The sound of the nuts falling into the water is said to make the sweetest music ever heard. There, the nuts are eaten by the five salmon living in the pool. The salmon separate the fruit of the nuts from their shells and send the shells down the five streams which lead off from the pool. Eventually it is revealed to Cormac that this is the Spring of Knowledge out of which flow the streams of the five senses "through which knowledge is obtained." Manannán says that to become one of the "people of many arts," one would have to drink both directly from the spring as well as from the streams.

Deities and Heroes

In the divine lore of Ireland, the C-few would correspond to the primeval God **Cian mac Cainte,** who is the father of Lugh Lamfadha. Among the Goddesses, it is the **Caillach,** or divine hag, who rules the year from Samhain to Beltaine. Caillach is a general title given to many of the primeval Goddesses of Ireland.

In the lore of the great Irish heroes, the C-few corresponds to **CúChulainn,** who is said to be the son of Lugh Lamfadha (or his incarnation). The myths of CúChulainn can be read in the whole Ulster Cycle found in *Ancient Irish Tales.*

Divinatory Meanings

The C-few represents the distillation of the pure and concentrated essence of anything—especially of knowledge. It is the essence of the use of language for communicative purposes, the mystery of how ideas are formed and realized in consciousness. It is from this ultimate source or spring that creative energy is produced. It is the essence of all truth and beauty.

In the oracular aspect, the C-few councils that you will either become the facilitator of self-discovery in others, or you will soon be the recipient of such teaching from someone else. You should concentrate on the acquisition of knowledge and wisdom. You may be the arbitrator of some conflict, or some conflict you are having will be mediated according to the principles of wisdom. The C-few says you should search for the source of all things.

There is mastery and skill being directed in a conscious way. The challenge of the hazel is that there may be a tendency not to follow intuition, and as a result creativity may be blocked. There will be a dissolution of talent and ability. You may be blocked by a fear of failure from within, or there may be blockages imposed from the outside.

Professions

Among the human arts, the C-few corresponds to the profession of harping and to that of musician in general.

The Fifths

Coll in Mide	Creativity in Sovereignty	ELOQUENCE (+)
Coll in Seis	Creativity in Harmony	BEAUTY (+)
Coll in Fis	Creativity in Learning	TEACHING (+)
Coll in Cath	Creativity in Conflict	ARBITRATION (+)
Coll in Blath	Creativity in Prosperity	ARTS (+)

APPLE

Divinatory Keywords

BEAUTY

ETERNITY

Queírt  Apple

(Pyrus malus)

The apple and the apple tree are potent symbols in Celtic lore. In Brythonic myth, it is associated with the Otherworld in the form of Avalon—the Island of Apples. In the tale of "Cormac's Adventures in the Land of Promise," we are told of a warrior (later revealed to be Manannán mac Lir) who had a silver branch from which hung three golden apples. This branch, called the craebh ciuil in Irish, made sweet music which inspired joy. It could heal the sick, and it could cause people to go to sleep if it were shaken toward them.

The apple in general is a sweet and healthy fruit. Its juice can be made into an alcoholic drink—which would make its symbolic links with the Underworld very strong.

Because when an apple is cut crosswise a fivefold pattern of the arrangement of its seeds is revealed in its core, the apple has been connected to the fivefold mathematical formula of the Pythagorean pentagram and the laws of proportion contained in the phi-ratio.

Deities and Heroes

In the sound system of the oghams, the Q-few was used as an alternate spelling for the C-sound. Therefore, as far as correspondences in the field of alliterative lists are concerned, the correspondences found with the C-few would also hold for *queirt*. Beyond this superficial situation, however, it can be said that the Q-few corresponds to a Hidden God, or Hidden Hero, who dwells—or slumbers—beyond the limits of human sensibilities. This figure awaits the hour of awakening.

Divinatory Meanings

The Q-few is a sign of beauty and eternity—a kind of eternal perfection and symmetry. The apple indicates eternal youthfulness and vitality even beyond death. It is the shelter of the deer as well as a sign of those who have gone mad because of visions of their own deaths. It is a vital link to the Underworld, and the depths of its fruit can only be enjoyed by those strong enough to withstand its sometimes subtle terrors.

The apple advises you to live fully and to seek beauty and perfection in all that you do. Efforts should be balanced, yet full of vigor. A healthy skepticism must be maintained, however. A lover may be a key to your quest.

The main challenge of *queirt* is the tendency to split attention. Energy tends to be scattered, loyalties are split off and one has a tendency to try to do too much at once. The challenge is to chose only one. Delusions (perhaps brought on by drugs or irrational subjectivity) could be a danger.

Professions

Among the professions ascribed to the ogham fews, *queirt* corresponds to the flute player or to all musicians in general. Here again is shows its linkage with the C-few. The "music" played by this musician may be of a mysterious sort—one played in the harmonies of various worlds and heard only in secret moments.

The Fifths

Queirt in Mide	Eternity in Sovereignty	PERFECTION (+)
Queirt in Seis	Eternity in Harmony	SATISFACTION (+)
Queirt in Fis	Eternity in Learning	ESOTERICA (+)
Queirt in Cath	Eternity in Conflict	DOUBT (−)
Queirt in Blath	Eternity in Prosperity	COMPLETION (+)

VINE

Divinatory Keyword

INWARDNESS

Muín  Víne

(Vitis vinifera)

 This originally refers to the grapevine, although other vine-like bushes or brambles might have been substituted for the name in Ireland. The grapevine was, of course, introduced to the British Isles from the continent. It required meticulous care in order for it to bear fruit. It was certainly something only enjoyed by the highest echelons of society for many centuries. The intricate interlacing vine motif in Celtic art is quite pronounced (as opposed to the zoomorphic interlace of Germanic art). The interlace is a sign of the intricacies of the subjective world made manifest and objective.

Deíties and Heroes

In the lore of the Irish Gods, it is to the God of the sea, **Manannán mac Lir Morfessa,** that the M-few corresponds. Manannán is the Lord of the Underworld—which lies below the sea. It is Manannán who shaped the Underworld realms of the *sídhe* for the Tuatha Dé Danann. Human consciousness as we perceive it is a weave of the consciousness derived from expe-

riences and memories of this world *(bith)* and those derived from the Underworld realm of Manannán.

It would also correspond to **Morfessa,** the "Master of Great Knowledge" who rules the Otherworldly City of Falias in the north.

Among the Goddesses, the M-few corresponds to the **Morrighan.** Her name literally means "the Great Queen," or perhaps "Queen of the Phantoms." She is the leader and embodiment of a Goddess-triad collectively called the *morrigu.* This triad also includes the war-Goddesses Nemain and Badb or Macha and Nemain. These are Goddesses of war and magic—and of certain kinds of eroticism. The Morrighan eventually finds expression in the Arthurian legends as Morgan le Fey.

In the heroic legends of Ireland, the M-few corresponds to **Mongan**—who is actually "son" or actually a rebirth or incarnation of Manannán mac Lir. It is also clear that Mongan was the incarnation of Fionn mac Cumhaill. In all events, Mongan is the archetype of the heroic human who braves the Underworld to gain magical knowledge.

Divinatory Meanings

The vine is a symbol of the intertwining of the conscious and unconscious mind. It is a sign of liberation from inhibitions restricting knowledge and actions. It is a gentle and systematic release from the constraints of logic and rationality. This liberation does not come through an abandonment of logic, or a drunken suppression of control, but through the full understanding of the interweaving—in the fashion of the vine—of the inner and outer, the upper and lower realms.

In a divinatory reading, the M-stave indicates that you will find some inner key to your problems, that they await an inspired solution. This may come from an unexpected quarter. You must be strong enough to be patient. In this, patience is great power. Await the truth shining from within, and from beyond. You may meet with a teacher.

You are challenged to follow your intuitive or inspired instincts. There is a danger, however, of becoming lost in your own subjective, intoxicating enthusiasms. Be careful not to become blind to objective truth. Another direction this challenge could take is the tendency to be overly self-critical. Be objective, but see your accomplishments for what they are as well.

Professions

The profession governed by the vine is that of soldiering—or that of the warrior. In a divinatory reading, it may refer to someone in a military profession, or to one who sees himself on the spiritual path of the warrior.

The Fifths

Muin in Mide	Inwardness in Sovereignty	Dignity (+)
Muin in Seis	Inwardness in Harmony	Subtlety (+)
Muin in Fis	Inwardness in Learning	Modesty (+)
Muin in Cath	Inwardness in Conflict	Pride (+)
Muin in Blath	Inwardness in Prosperity	Prestige (+)

IVY

Divinatory Keyword

DEVELOPMENT

Gort  Ivy

(Hedra helix)

The ivy is an extremely hardy plant and can grow to a great age. When this happens, the trunk can be as wide as a foot in diameter. The plant will grow out in all directions, climbing up any vertical surface and out over all flat planes in a tenacious manner.

The ivy is especially seen as a sign of femininity in the British Isles. The archaic carol "The Holly and the Ivy" refers to the eternal conflict between the sexes—the holly being a strongly masculine tree.

Deities and Heroes

In the divine lore of the Irish, the G-few corresponds to the great Smith-God, **Goibhniu.** Among the Cymru, this was **Gwydion,** the shoemaker. The Celts were renowned as metal-workers from very ancient times. Their smiths had reputations very much akin to those of medieval alchemists. Their art was that of the transformation of substances from the base into

the divine, from the useless into the precious. The Cymric linguistic equivalent of Goibhniu is Gofannon, who was the Cymric God of Smithcraft, but whose exploits have largely been lost to us.

Divinatory Meanings

There is a fierce and determined power in the G-few. It gives the boar-like tenacity to apply the will to do difficult and intricate work. The ivy is a sign of the development and transformation of the self.

In divination, this few indicates that you may soon be involved in a change in your educational or business life, and there are perhaps some gains to be had in connection with it. However, the path is also fraught with pitfalls. There may be those who are envious of your accomplishments. Seek the best of guidance in what you do in matters touched by the G-few.

The main challenge of *gort* is not to get caught up in the tools of the transformative process. Remember that the tools are not the ends, but only means to give rise to something emerging from the depths of your psyche. Keep your focus on your true goals. There is the danger of falling into ruts of psychological behavior. Seek the original and unique to overcome this tendency.

Professions

Occupations having to do with metalwork or perhaps nowadays chemistry or anything having to do with the manipulation and transformation of natural substances corresponds to the G-few. Persons fitting this description may also be indicated in a divinatory reading.

The Fifths

Gort in Mide	Development in Sovereignty	DEVELOPMENT (+)
Gort in Seis	Development in Harmony	ATTAINMENT (+)
Gort in Fis	Development in Learning	EDUCATION (+)
Gort in Cath	Development in Conflict	RUIN (−)
Gort in Blath	Development in Prosperity	FUTILITY (−)

REED

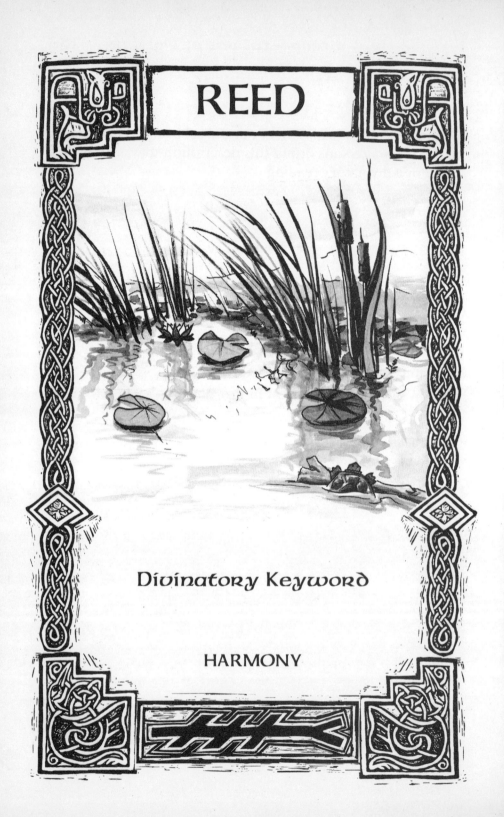

Divinatory Keyword

HARMONY

Ngetal  Reed (Broom)

(Various types)

There is some variation in the traditions surrounding this oghamic character. The name may refer to the common reed (of the genus *Phragmites* or *Arundo)* or to the broom *(Cytisus scoparius)*. In the Brythonic or Cymric tradition, the sound-value was changed to the P-sound, and it was given the name *peith,* whitten. In all events, the plant is one noted for its straight and flexible stems.

The NG-few is an archaic vestige of the original oghamic series which predates the sound systems of either Irish or Cymric. The fact that it remains as a part of the system, however, is a testament to the highly conservative nature of the tradition.

Deities and Heroes

There are no Irish Gods or Goddesses with their names beginning with this ogham character. Those corresponding to the N-few could be used here.

Divinatory Meanings

The reed is a plant which grows straight up out of a marshy and wet land near the sea or lakes. In the NG-few, there is the union of complementary opposites. It is the roaring of the sea—the dynamism of that which is forever steady. It is that aspect of the Celtic Otherworld which has to do with the subtle union between the conscious world and the unconscious reality existing side by side with that which we perceive. There is something essential about how the arts are understood and practiced which is housed in the NG-few. It is a sign of growth and good health.

The *ngetal* is a sign of harmony between this realm and those beyond it. There is a unity of purpose and will. Inner direction and outer manifestation seem to flow together in a harmonious fashion. There is a high level of ability to adapt and modify things to your will and purpose.

The main challenge of the NG-few is that you may be distracted by the beauties along the way to such an extent that you forget the purpose of the journey of transformation. There may also be a great deal of inner turmoil and anxiety manifesting in your life. The solution is to be found in a sense of purpose and direction.

Professions

The traditional profession associated with the NG-few is "modeling" (O.Ir. *ngibae* or *gebech*) which might better be understood as "designing." This is the activity of creating something in the mind before it is executed in the manifest universe. This few rules artistic creativity and those with the ability to envision that which they will fashion. This faculty is necessary in many types of work and play. It is the faculty of the imagination. Almost all creative people partake of the power of the NG-few.

The Fifths

Ngetal in Mide	Harmony in Sovereignty	STABILITY (+)
Ngetal in Seis	Harmony in Harmony	HARMONY (+)
Ngetal in Fis	Harmony in Learning	BEAUTY (+)
Ngetal in Cath	Harmony in Conflict	REST (+)
Ngetal in Blath	Harmony in Prosperity	GOOD MANNERS (+)

BLACKTHORN

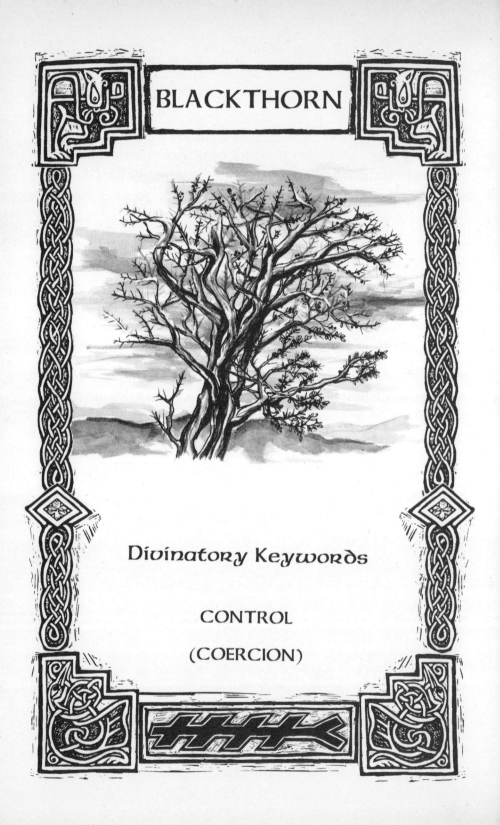

Divinatory Keywords

CONTROL

(COERCION)

Straif  Blackthorn

(Prunus spinosa)

 The blackthorn is generally considered to be a plant bearing bad luck or to be an expression of forces detrimental to normal humankind, but, esoterically, it has its useful side as well.

The blackthorn is known as the "black rod" or blasting rod of malevolent magicians or witches. It is often seen in the form of a walking stick—which is also used as a club or weapon. The blackthorn is the tree of malevolent magic as the hazel is that of the benevolent sort.

Whereas the yew is also a deadly plant, the yew works on a more straightforward level. This is symbolized by the use of the yew in the making of bows to shoot arrows or to fashion the hilts of daggers. The blackthorn, on the other hand, is often used as the magical weapon to wound effigies of one's enemies.

Deities and Heroes

There are no Irish Gods or Goddesses with names beginning with this ogham character. Those corresponding to the S-few could be used here.

Divinatory Meanings

In the main, the blackthorn is a sign of external control; that is, a control exerted from the outside on a person or thing. This is usually an unwanted sort of control, but not always. Besides, this ability or power is oftentimes the operative principle of magic. The key then becomes learning how to make use of this force without being used by it.

This may be taken as council to make use of magical means to deal with a problem, but it more likely is trying to indicate that there are forces at work which are compelling and controlling you from beyond your present level of understanding. These may be forces from deep within you, or from without. They are probably not beneficial, however, as they are presently being made manifest in your life.

You may be under the control of forces beyond your grasp. The main challenge in the Z-few is the necessity of turning what might be an initially negative experience into a positive one—through knowledge and understanding. The key is to be found in not striving against the experience, but directing the energy produced to positive ends. Here can be the beginning of true spiritual understanding. The solution to a problem bound up with the blackthorn may be to play it away—much as a child might exorcise inner anxieties—and even learn to indulge in them.

Professions

Among the professions, the Z-few corresponds to the "deer-stalker" (O. Ir. *sreghuindeacht);* that is, the hunter. In modern times, this skill may be incorporated in the business world with those who seek and cunningly obtain advantage for themselves. In a divinatory reading, it may indicate someone with these characteristics.

The Fifths

Straif in Mide	Control in Sovereignty	STEWARDSHIP (+)
Straif in Seis	Control in Harmony	VEHEMENCE (−)
Straif in Fis	Control in Learning	TESTING (−)
Straif in Cath	Control in Conflict	CAPTURE (−)
Straif in Blath	Control in Prosperity	DEBT (−)

ELDER

Divinatory Keyword

CHANGE

Ruís  Elder

(Sambucus nigra)

The elder is considered to be a bad tree to be burned for fuel, although the hollow stems of its young branches were typically used as kindling. Burning it indoors was thought to "bring the Devil" into the house. (This may derive from the obviously later belief that the cross upon which Jesus was crucified was made of elder wood.)

The red color derived from the berries of this tree was used cosmetically to simulate a blushing effect on the cheeks. In the oghamic lore, the most often mentioned characteristic of *ruis* has to do with this blushing for shame, considered as a positive sign or trait.

Deities and Heroes

Among the Gods of Ireland, the one who corresponds most powerfully to the *ruis* is **Ruadh Rofessa**—"the Red-one who knows all." This is an alternate name for the Dagda, the Good-

God. Among the Goddesses, it corresponds to **Rigru Roiscle-than,** who is an Otherworldly queen and divinity of Irish sovereignty. In common Celtic mythology, the R-few corresponds to the Goddess **Rigantona**—whose name simply means "the great queen." This title is best given to **Rhiannon,** who is the equine Goddess and daughter of the King of the Underworld.

In the heroic mythology of Ireland, the R-few corresponds to **Ragallach,** an early king of the land who received a prophesy that he would die at his daughter's hand. When he had a daughter, he therefore ordered her killed. However, she survived to later become the concubine of her own father. This illustrates the twists of fate inherent in the R-few.

Divinatory Meanings

The R is a sign of evolutionary change, of a transition from one state of being to another. If understood, the realization of the mystery of this few will lead to a balanced and mature outlook on life.

Old things are passing away; new things will take their place. These will be a passage of some kind, perhaps a trip or a change in domicile. There may be a change in your health. There is a need to be able to let go of things that are holding you back.

The chief challenge of the *ruis* is the necessity of coming to terms with the endless cycles of changes. All things will undergo evolutionary changes and therefore will eventually pass away. This must be seen and understood. But there may also be a tendency to stagnate if these changes are not allowed to happen.

Professions

Among the traditional ancient Irish professions, the R-few corresponds to "dispensing" (O.Ir. *ronairecht*). This is the activity of dispensing or distributing what others have created. It is the oghamic character of the "middle man"—the one whose abilities make what others have created available to a wider audience or public.

The Fifths

Ruis in Mide	Change in Sovereignty	MATURITY (+)
Ruis in Seis	Change in Harmony	NEW KNOWLEDGE (+)
Ruis in Fis	Change in Learning	ADVANCEMENT (+)
Ruis in Cath	Change in Conflict	SURVIVAL (+)
Ruis in Blath	Change in Prosperity	GENEROSITY (+)

FIR

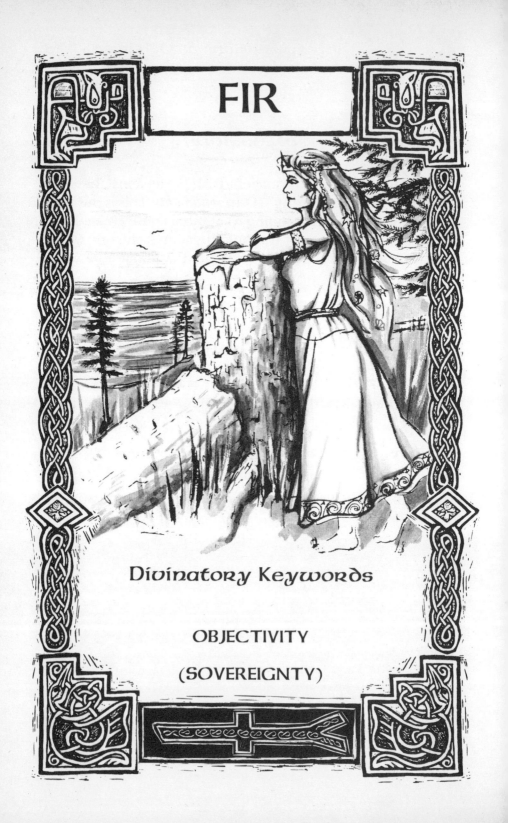

Divinatory Keywords

OBJECTIVITY

(SOVEREIGNTY)

Ailm  Fír

(Trees of the genus Abies)

The silver fir is considered by many to be a tree denoting birth or the beginning of things. It stands at the head of the series of vowels in the ogham system, while the yew (considered by many to be a tree of "death") stands at the end of that series.

In the Orkney Islands, it was a custom to bless a newborn baby and its mother by going around the bed containing them with a torch made of a fir-wood. Interestingly, the Irish used the word *ailm* to translate the name of the Mediterranean palm tree—which is the tree of nativity in that region.

Deities and Heroes

Among the ancient Gods of the Celts, one of the most ancient is **Aedh,** the primeval Fire-God. He is the embodiment of the sacrificial fires ignited at the great Celtic fire-festivals such as Samhain and Beltaine. **Aine** is a form of the Goddess of the Sovereignty of Ireland, who is either the wife or daughter of

the Sea-God, Manannán mac Lir. In these two figures, Aedh and Aine, there is the primeval dichotomy between fire and water.

In the heroic mythology of Ireland, the A-few most closely corresponds to **Art,** who is one of the traditional kings of Ireland. He was supposed to have reigned from 220 to 254 CE, but tales concerning him are obviously mythic in character. "The Adventures of Art Son of Conn" can be found in *Ancient Irish Tales*. His adventures are prime examples of the socio-magical role of sovereignty in ancient Celtic tradition.

Divinatory Meanings

The A indicates a transformation from a weak state into a strong one. It is a sign of good health and strength. It is a raw, basic force of health and vigor. This is a highly elevated state of being. From the height of this perspective, objectivity is gained and wisdom is found as a result of the objectivity. The A is the beginning of the path to finding truth and life—just as the final few in this *aicme* is the end of life and the final truth.

In divinatory readings, the *ailm* indicates that there is a great transformation for the better in the offing. Strength will be gathered and new insights and objectivity gained. There may be an opportunity to exercise a sovereign power in the near future.

One of the chief challenges inherent in this few is that the subject of a divinatory reading may be challenged to exercise power in a sovereign way without the benefit of full maturity or objectivity. This can be a very painful experience.

Professions

Among the traditional arts or professions, this few corresponds to "kingship" or sovereignty (O.Ir. *airigeacht*). This does not only refer to kings as such, but also to those who exercise a sovereign power in their societies or businesses. This few may, of course, also refer to a person of this type in a divinatory reading.

The Fifths

Ailm in Mide	Objectivity in Sovereignty	SOVEREIGNTY (+)
Ailm in Seis	Objectivity in Harmony	DISCOVERY (+)
Ailm in Fis	Objectivity in Learning	MASTERY (+)
Ailm in Cath	Objectivity in Conflict	STRATEGY (+)
Ailm in Blath	Objectivity in Prosperity	ORIGINALITY (+)

FURZE

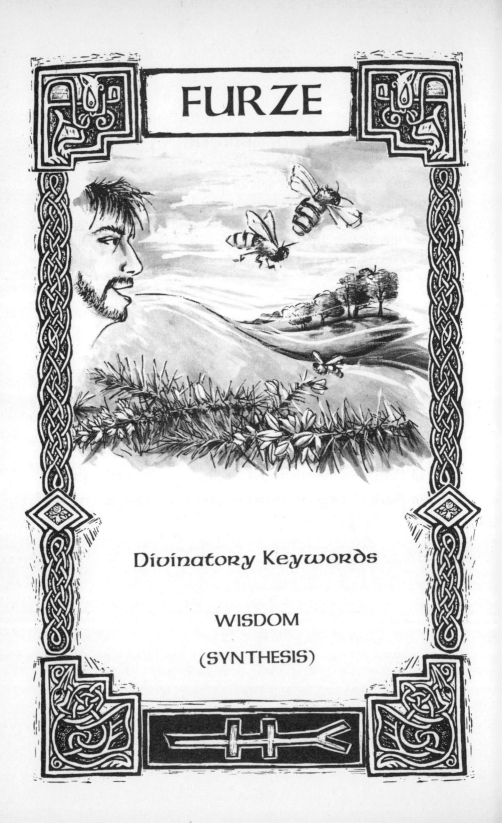

Divinatory Keywords

WISDOM

(SYNTHESIS)

Onn

Furze
(Gorse)

(Ulex europaeus)

The gorse or furze is a low growing shrub with long, threadlike spines. It is an evergreen, but its leaves often fall off and are very small. Its most outstanding feature is its small, fragrant, yellow-golden blossoms. There is an old saying: "When the gorse is out of bloom, kissing's out of season." This reflects a British custom of placing a spray of gorse in the bridal bouquet.

The gorse makes a fine food for animals—especially after it has either been ground into meal for horses, or after it has been burned on the hillsides for the sheep to eat. The effect of both processes, of grinding or burning, is to destroy the hard thorns— leaving only the tender shoots.

Deities and Heroes

In the lore of the Gods of Ireland, it is **Ogma** who corresponds to the sound of the O-few. His mythology is covered in

chapter 1. He is the God of the strength of eloquence and the might of linguistic faculties. His is the power of the spoken and written word.

Oisin is the hero classified by the O-few. He is the son of Fionn and Sàbh. He was a bard (or more technically a *fili*)—a master of the word—and a member of the Fianna. This was the Irish band of warrior poets (akin to the Teutonic Erulians). Oisin spent 300 years in the Land of Youth with his Otherworldly lover Niamh. When he returned from the Underworld on an otherworldly horse given to him by Niamh, he was not to let his foot touch the ground on this side. But the girth of the horse slipped and his foot touched the ground, whereupon he became an aged man. Oisin related the history of the Fianna to St. Patrick that it might be recorded in words for the ages.

Divinatory Meanings

The furze is a sign of the in-gathering of sweet and valuable things. One of its other symbols is that of the beehive. Bees create honey—an ancient symbol of wisdom because it is a sweet substance which comes only after hard work. This is the gathering together—or synthesis—of valuable things (material, information, people or whatever) for a great purpose. This is one of the main functions of a chieftain or sovereign.

Now may be a time to sit back and gather yourself and the things around you together in order to come to a new and higher understanding—which is wisdom. There may be some influence from a divine source if you are open to it. Your way will be eased in life by a period of active internal synthesis. Get yourself together within your own self. This will, of course, perhaps lead to a radical change in your approach to life and to matters surrounding any individual question.

The main challenge associated with the O-few would be the tendency to scatter focus and concentration because too much attention is given to the very activity of gathering information or material. You must act effectively to meet the sovereign aim. Also, there may be some difficulty in gathering something you need.

Professions

The work traditionally ascribed to this few is harvesting (O.Ir. *ogmoracht*). This refers to the act of working with a thing, cultivating it and eventually seeing it come to fruition—and then making use of it.

The Fifths

Onn in Mide	Wisdom in Sovereignty	GUIDANCE (+)
Onn in Seis	Wisdom in Harmony	RULERSHIP (+)
Onn in Fis	Wisdom in Learning	PASSION (+)
Onn in Cath	Wisdom in Conflict	CHANGE (+)
Onn in Blath	Wisdom in Prosperity	SECURITY (+)

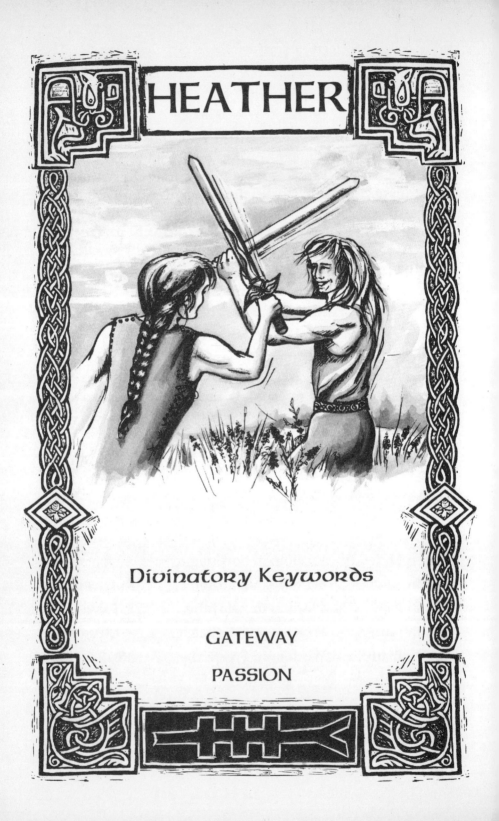

HEATHER

Divinatory Keywords

GATEWAY

PASSION

Ur  Heather

(Calluna vulgaris)

Red heather at midsummer is a sign of passion and is associated with the mountains and with acts of passion. The white heather is a protection against acts of passion and is considered a lucky sign. Both are attractive to bees and are thus associated with the sovereign work of the spirit and with vigorous activity.

Heather grows widely over the land in Ireland and Britain. In Wales "heather ale" is brewed as a restorative—and it would seem that such brews have their origins in very archaic periods when such drinks had a sacred purpose.

Deities and Heroes

In the divine mythology, the U-few answers to the name of the master of wisdom, **Uscias,** who dwelt in the Otherworldly city of Findias in the south. He gave the sword to the God Nuadu.

Uathach was the daughter of Scathach, who taught the

greatest Irish hero CúChulainn the arts of war. Uathach allowed CúChulainn to join Scathach's "school." She later became his mistress after he killed her lover. This shows both the gateway aspect of the few (through her, CúChulainn gains entry) and the aspect of passion.

Divinatory Meanings

This is the sign of romance and dreams. In the U-few, there is a strong connection between the conscious self of the subject and the deep levels of his or her unconscious. The *ur* is a gateway between the inner world and the outer one. In the U, there is the expression of the need for passion and ecstasy in life.

When the *ur* turns up in a divinatory reading, the subject is usually being advised to find gateways to passion in life—or there may be such an opening coming in the future. The influences of imagination, intuition and dreams are very strong.

The main challenges of the U-few are the tendency to see projects and direction dissolve under futile attempts to realize them. There may be some betrayal by people close to you. Do not be caught in the trap of merely dreaming. Act on your passions—but act wisely.

Professions

In the tradition of the Old Irish professions as ascribed to the ogham fews, U corresponds to "brasswork" *(umaideacht)*. This refers to the skill of metalwork—of transformation of valuable natural substances—as applied in the more refined or domestic arts. This can be compared to, and contrasted with, the harder, more warrior-like aspects of the smithwork found with the G-few.

The Fifths

Ur in Mide	Passion in Sovereignty	INSPIRATION (+)
Ur in Seis	Passion in Harmony	DISTURBANCE (−)
Ur in Fis	Passion in Learning	EAGERNESS (+)
Ur in Cath	Passion in Conflict	FURY (+)
Ur in Blath	Passion in Prosperity	GREED (−)

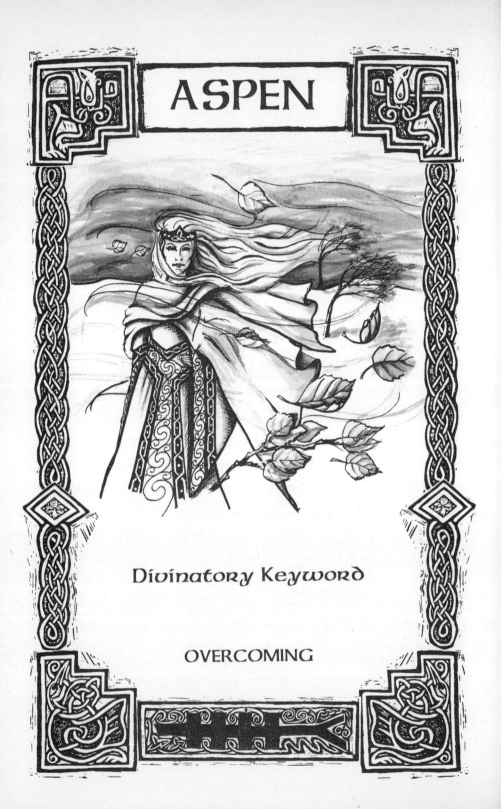

ASPEN

Divinatory Keyword

OVERCOMING

Edad  Aspen

(Populus tremuloides)

This tree is the aspen or white poplar. In ancient Celtic times, shields were often made from the wood of the aspen. Ancient bards would also sometimes divine by means of listening to the sounds made by the wind rushing through the leaves of the poplar. (In the "Old English Rune-Poem" the tree described under the b-rune *(beorc)* is really the aspen or poplar.)

It was the custom of ancient Irish coffin makers to have a measuring stick, called a *fe*. This was always made of aspen wood and was used to measure the body for its coffin as well as the grave to be dug for it. The esoteric significance of the aspen wood as to point to the overcoming of death.

Deities and Heroes

In the divine mythology, the E-few answers to the name of the master of wisdom, **Esras,** who dwelt in the Otherworldly city of

Gorias in the east. He gave a spear to the God Lugh.

Among the Goddesses, the *edad* closely corresponds to **Eriu,** who is the personification of the power of sovereignty. It is from this name that the island gets its name. The name is also cognate to the first element in the names Ir-an, and Ar-yan, as well as the Germanic Irmen (or Yrmin). All have to do with those who execute sovereign powers.

In the heroic mythology, this few is linked to **Emer,** the true wife of CúChulainn. Her father sent the hero to train with Scathach to become worthy of his daughter. She was, however, always jealous of CúChulainn's many other attachments with women. She was especially jealous of Fand, an Otherworldly woman. Eventually Emer was given a magical drink to make her forget her jealousy.

Divinatory Meanings

Edad is a sign of determination in the face of negativity. It is a sign of actually being able to overcome the negative situation through a welling up of inner reserves and strength. There is resistance—but it is overcome. This is a sign of protection against foes.

In divinatory readings, the E-few generally indicates that there may be some adversity in your everyday life, but that you will probably have the inner strength to overcome it—but the source of this strength must be within. You are advised to seek in some creative way for the source of this strength, to come to know it and to make it manifest in your life.

The challenge of *edad* is the tendency to give in to the forces that oppose us, or to burdens which tend to overwhelm us—especially those of which we remain unconscious. Be aware of this challenge.

Professions

Among the traditional professions of old Ireland, the E-few corresponds to "fowling," or bird hunting. This refers to the skills of cunning and patience. This few may also refer to persons especially gifted these virtues.

The Fifths

Edad in Mide	Overcoming in Sovereignty	OVERCOMING (+)
Edad in Seis	Overcoming in Harmony	COMPLETION (+)
Edad in Fis	Overcoming in Learning	DISCIPLINE (+)
Edad in Cath	Overcoming in Conflict	FORCE (+)
Edad in Blath	Overcoming in Prosperity	CRAFT (+)

YEW

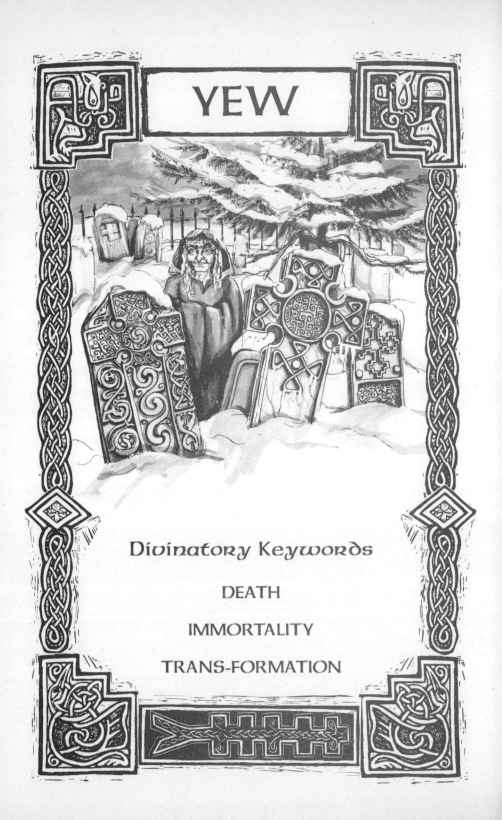

Divinatory Keywords

DEATH

IMMORTALITY

TRANS-FORMATION

Idad  Yew

(Taxus baccata)

In the tree-lore of the ancient northern peoples, only the oak and perhaps the ash are as storied as the yew. Yew wood is extremely hard, and the trees themselves live to great ages. Some in the British Isles today are around 2,000 years old. Many of these are to be found in churchyards—formerly heathen sacred sites of the Celts and the Anglo-Saxons alike. Because of this, the yew is a perfect symbol of eternity. It is also a powerful symbol of life and death because it is an evergreen tree—alive when all else is dead around it, yet poisonous; its fruit can cause death.

As a postscript to the Irish tale of the ill-fated elopement of Naoisi and Deidre, after the lovers had tragically died, the Ulstermen, who wished to keep them apart in life, attempted to do so in death by having yew stakes driven through the lovers' bodies when they were buried. However, the yew stakes grew into trees and eventually reached up and arched together over the cathedral at Armagh.

Deities and Heroes

An alternate name of Lugh Lamfadha, **Ildanach,** which means "the many gifted," might best be applied to the I-few. He is shown to deserve this name in the tale of "The Second Battle of Magh Tured," where he lists all of his many talents (*Ancient Irish Tales*, 35-36). For this, he is also called the Samildanach, or "many talented." This aspect sums up the all-encompassing nature of the final ogham character.

Among the divine female figures of Ireland, the yew might be associated with **Irnan,** who was a magical hag sister killed by the hero Goll of the Fianna when she challenged any of the warrior band to fight her. Here the aspect of the "death of death" is emphasized.

Divinatory Meanings

This is the essence of the self—that which is inherited from the ancestral past. It is the eternal root of the self. This becomes the central reference point by which time and life are measured. This reference point is also the ultimate measure of the passage of the soul from life to life. Often the outward manifestation of this will be the innate talents or abilities passed from one generation to another—often skipping one or more generations.

In divinatory readings, the I-few usually refers to transformation or movement of some kind. Here, death is understood as a kind of transformation from one state of being to another. This is very often fraught with discomfort and a sense of loss. If, however, these transformations are experienced in a conscious state—a state of sovereigntythey will be seen and understood for what they are. There is a high likelihood that this few will indicate that there is either ignorance of a certain forthcoming transformation, or it is indicating that awareness of such a metamorphosis is immanent.

The chief challenge of the yew is the inner feeling of loss and sorrow which often accompanies transformations of all kinds. There will be grief to be worked through before the change will be fully understood.

Professions

Among the traditional professions, the I-few corresponds to both fishing and working in yew wood. In contemporary terms, these could be seen to correspond to any skills in which patience and precision are needed and valued.

The Fifths

Idad in Mide	Death in Sovereignty	TRANSFORMATION (+)
Idad in Seis	Death in Harmony	DISCORD (−)
Idad in Fis	Death in Learning	DISILLUSION (−)
Idad in Cath	Death in Conflict	FEAR (−)
Idad in Blath	Death in Prosperity	LOSS/GRIEF (−)

Afterword

True *divination* is more than fortune telling. Oghamic divination is a means of gaining access to deep transpersonal structures and patterns of existence. By working toward gaining access to these structures and patterns, the potential bard is working toward an understanding of things not only embedded deep within the *self* but also deeply submerged in the profound realms of archetypal history.

The contemporary bard, like the ancient counterparts of that office, must have the tools to *read* his or her way into the deep well of eternity. The bard must be able to drink from the streams of the five senses as well as from the well of Conla and blend these essences within the self before true wisdom can be reached; that is, the outer forms of the ogham characters and their various symbols must be synthesized with the actual internal and eternal forms of which they are but reflections. There true wisdom begins.

In the traditional kind of understanding presented in this system, the potential bard has the opportunity to delve into the depths of the traditional world of the ancient Celts in a way never before possible. If the apprentice bard works diligently at both theoretically *understanding* and practically *reading* the true oghams, not only will he or she be opened up to a remarkable inner wisdom but h or she will also be given a gateway to the keys to the objective living mysteries of the ancient Celts. The oghams can make the ancient tales and myths, the facts of Celtic history, come alive from *within* the experience of the bard. Once this takes place, the Celtic twilight will again give way to a true Celtic dawn.

—Edred Thorsson
Austin, Texas
Oimelc, 1990

197

Oghamic
Table of Correspondences

I No.	II Shape	III Sound Value	IV Tree Name	V Translation of Tree-Name
1		B	beith	birch
2		L	luis	rowan
3		F	fern	alder
4		S	sail	willow
5		N	nin	ash
6		H	huath	whitethorn
7		D	duir	oak
8		T	tinne	holly
9		C	coll	hazel
10		QU	queirt	apple
11		M	muin	vine
12		G	gort	ivy
13		NG	ngetal	broom
14		ST	straif	blackthorn
15		R	ruis	elder

I No.	II Shape	III Sound Value	IV Tree Name	V Translation of Tree-Name
16		A	ailm	fir
17		O	onn	furze
18		U	ur	heather
19		E	edad	aspen
20		I	idad	yew

V Inner Meaning	VI Colors* (O.Ir.)	VII Translation of Colors
1 Vitality	*ban*	white
2 Insight/Quickening	*liath*	gray
3 Foundation	*flann*	red
4 Intuition	*sodath*	fine-colored
5 Rebirth	*necht*	clear
6 Misfortune	*huath*	"terrible"
7 Endurance	*dub*	black
8 Balance	*temen*	dark gray
9 Creativity	*cron*	brown
10 Beauty/Eternity	*quair*	mouse-colored
11 Inwardness	*mbracht*	varigated
12 Development	*gorm*	blue
13 Harmony	*nglas*	green
14 Control	*sorcha*	bright
15 Change	*ruadh*	red
16 Objectivity	*alad*	piebald
17 Wisdom/Synthesis	*odhar*	dun
18 Gateway/Passion	*usgdha*	resinous
19 Overcoming	*erc*	red
20 Death/Immortality	*irfind*	very white

VIII Birds	IX Translation of Bird-Names	X Arts and Crafts	XI Translation of Arts
1 *besan*	pheasant	*bethumnacht*	livelihood
2 *lachan*	duck	*lumnacht*	pilotage
3 *faelinn*	gull	*filideacht*	poetry
4 *seg*	hawk	*sairsi*	handicraft
5 *naescu*	snipe	*notaireacht*	notary work
6 *hadaig*	night raven	*h-airchetul*	trisyllabic poetry
7 *droen*	wren	*druidheacht*	wizardry
8 *truith*	starling	*tornoracht*	turning
9		*cruitireacht*	harping
10 *querc*	hen	*quislenacht*	fluting
11 *mintan*	titmouse	*milaideacht*	soldiering
12 *geis*	swan	*gaibneacht*	smithwork
13 *ngeigh*	goose	*ngibae*	modelling
14 *stmolach*	thrush	*sreghuindeacht*	deer stalking
15 *rocnat*	small rook	*ronaireacht*	dispensing
16 *aidhircleog*	lapwing	*airigeacht*	sovereignty
17 *odoroscrach*	scrat (?)	*ogmoracht*	harvesting
18 *uiseog*	lark	*umaideacht*	brasswork
19 *ela*	swan	*enaireacht*	fowling
20 *illait*	eaglet	(1) *iascaireacht* (2) *ibroracht*	(1) fishing (2) yew woodwork

*Note that the *Book of Ballymote* also contains a section called "Sow Ogham," which ascribes a color to each of the five vertical columns so that the first character in each *aicme* is white, the second is gray, the third is black, the fourth is amber and the fifth is blue.

The Table of
the Nemnivus Alphabet

Shape	Sound	Name	Trans. of Name	Runic model	Origin of Name
	a	altar	need		OE *nyd*, need
	b	braut			
	c	cusil	counsel		
	d	dexu			Welsh *derw*, oak
	e	egui			
	f	fich			
	g	guichr	torch		OE *cen*, torch
	h	huil			
	i	iechuit			
	k	kam			
	l	louber	day		OE *dæg*, day
	m	muin	gift		OE *gyfu*, gift
	n	nihn			O.Ir. *nin*, ash
	o	or			
	p	parth			OE *perodh* (=p)
	q	quith			

Shape	Sound	Name	Trans. of Name	Runic model	Origin of Name
ᛩ	r	rat	joy	ᚱ	OE *wyn*, joy
ᚲ	s	surg			
ᛣ	t	traus		↑	
ᛅ	u	uir		ᚾ	OE *ur*, urox
ᛉ	z	zeirc			

Pronunciation of Old Irish

Irish is a difficult language to pronounce correctly because the ways the words are written often bear little resemblance to the ways they would seem to be pronounced from an English perspective. However, once some practice and familiarity with the spelling system is gained, it will be found to be easier than it might have appeared at first.

Most readers will have seen certain Irish words in at least two different spelling systems. For example, one might see "Samain" in one place and "Samhain" in another. The former is the true Old Irish orthography, while the latter is a more modern spelling in which the letter "h" has been added to indicate the special pronunciation of the "m" as a "w" or "v" sound. The pronunciation of both remains [saw-en].

Vowels

á = ah of *father*
a as above but shorter
é as in *they*
e as in *get*
í as "ee" in *greet*
i as in *hit*
ó as in *go*
o as in *hot*
ú as oo in *food*
u as u in *full*
ai = a in first syllable, and i elsewhere
iu = u with i only slightly sounded

ui = i but with the u slightly sounded
ei = e

Diphthongs

ae, ai, oe, oi = aw + ee; similar to the sound of oy in *boy* and the -igh in *high*

Here are the pronunciations of the consonants according to their position in words— whether the first letter, in the middle of a word or in final position.

Letter	Initial	Medial	Final
c	as k	as g	as g
p	as p	as b	as b
b	as b	as v or w	as v or w
d	as d	as th in *this*	as th in *this*
t	as t	as d	as d
g	hard as in get	as a gargled gh	as medial
m	m (very nasal)	as mv (nasal)	as medial

Consonants are *slender* when an e or i precedes or follows. Consonants which are *aspirated* are sometimes spelled with either a dot above them or with an h immediately after them.

Aspirated Consonants

ch = the guttural ch of *loch*; when slender as the ch in German *ich*
ph = as f in *fun*, "fy" sound as in *feud* when slender
th = th in *think* (silent in more modern Irish)
fh   this is silent, but sometimes it is a faint breathing
sh = as the h in *hit*; when slender, it sounds like the h in *hue*.

Unaspirated Consonants

f as in English, as "fy" sound in *feud* when slender
s as in *sing*, never as in *roses*; but, when followed by or pre-
    ceding an "e" or "i," as the "sh" in *shoe*
r trilled r as in Scottish pronunciation
ng as in *singer*, not as in *finger*
mb = mm; this sound is also sometimes spelled mm
nd = nn; this sound is also sometimes spelled nn
l as in *lay*
h is often silent or pronounced as a faint breathing sound.

Examples of most of the variations in Old Irish pronunciation
are given in the phonetic transcriptions of the words given in
the glossary.

Glossary

In the phonetic transcriptions of the Irish words and names which follow, the spelling dh = the "th" as in "then."

aicme [acme]: A family or group of five oghamic fews.

Beltaine [BELT-en-a]: Major Celtic vernal fire festival. Modern "May-Eve."

bith [bith]: The world, or the manifest physical universe.

blath [blath]: Prosperity. A quality describing the eastern realm among the Fifths.

Book of Ballymote: A 14th-century Irish manuscript containing the greatest collection of ogham lore of any O.Ir. text.

cath [cath]: Conflict. A quality describing the northern realm among the Fifths.

Caillach [kahll-ya*kh* or kell-ey]: Common name for the divine hag in Irish lore.

Dagda [doy-da]: The good god. The god of the Druids.

ebad [evadh]: Name of the *forfidh* corresponding to the sovereign center (*mide*). Its sound value is *ea* and its name menas "aspen." This is also another name for the E-few: An Anglicized form of the Irish *fidh*.

fianna [FEE-enna]: A wandering band of warrior-bards. Their most famous leader was Fionn mac Cumhaill. They correspond to the Erulian bands in Teutonic tradition.

fidh, pl. *fedha* [fidh; fedha]: Irish word for "wood,' or "tree" used to denote the oghamic characters—as well as the trees they represent.

Fifth: A "province" of the land or cosmos. Irish *coiced*, a fifth.

fis [fish]: Learning. A quality describing the western realm among the Fifths.

fili, pl. *filid* [filee; fileedh]: The Irish term which answers most closely to the term "Druid."

flesc [flesk]: The stemline.

forfidh, pl. *forfedha* [for-fidh; for-fedha]: The additional five fews which are used for diphthongs, and which are used to symbolize the five provinces.

geis, *pl. geisa* [gay-sh, gay-sha]: A kind of "taboo" in Celtic lore which is typically a prohibition against doing something, but which is at the same time a source of power.

iphin [ifin]: Name of the *forfidh* corresponding to the north (*cath*). Its sound value is *io* and its name means "gooseberry."

Lugh [lu*gh* or loo]: The Celtic god of magic, war, and the arts. His emblematic weapon is the spear. In many ways he answers to the Teutonic god Wóden.

mag (or *magh*) [moy]: A plane or field. Used of the higher or "Otherworlds."

midhe [midh-e]: "The Middle." See also *rige*.

Morrighan: "The Great Queen," or "Queen of Phantoms."

morrighna [mor-ri*gh*na]: A collective name for the three-aspected form of Morrighan, which also includes Nemain and either Badh or Macha.

nemeton: Celtic term for a sacred grove and enclosure.

notch: The short lines or dots used to indicate the vowels of the oghamic system.

oir [or]: Name of the *forfidh* corresponding to the south (*seis*). Its name means "spindle."

Ogma: The Irish hero whose name is represented in the name of the oghamic system. He is the Irish Hercules. Gaulish form of his name is Ogimos.

Otherworld: A collective name for the celestial or "higher" realm(s) in the Celtic cosmology. These are most often designated with names with the Irish word *magh* (plane) in them.

phagos [faghos]: Name of the *forfidh* corresponding to the east (*blath*). Originally this seems to have been a Greek word. Its sound value is *ae* and its name means "beech."

rige [ree-a]: Sovereignty. A quality describing the middle realm or the *mide* of the Fifths.

Samhain (also **Samain**) [saw-en]: "The End of Summer," the major Celtic autumnal fire festival. Modern "Hallowe'en."

score: The lines which cross the stemline to form the oghamic fews.

seis [shesh]: Harmony. A quality describing the southern realm among the Fifths.

sídhe (or *sid*) [shee]: The realm of the dead, the "fairy realm," or the Underworld in Celtic lore.

stemline: The straight line on which the notches and scores are cut to make the ogham fews.

tír [teer]: This word generally means "land," but also is used symbolically for names of the "Underworld."

uileand [ulen]: Name of the *forfidh* corresponding to the west (*fis*). Its name means "honeysuckle."

Underworld: A collective name for the chthonic or "lower" realm(s) in the Celtic cosmology. These are most often designated with names with the Irish word *tír* (land) in them.

Bibliography

Calder, G. *Auraicept na N'Eces.* Edinbuugh: John Grant, 1917.

Caesar, Julius. *The Conquest of Gaul.* Harmondsworth, UK: Penguin, 1951.

Chadwick, Nora. *The Celts.* Harmondsworth, UK: Penguin, 1970.

Cross, Tom P. and Slover, Clark H., eds. *Ancient Irish Tales.* Dublin: Figgis, 1936.

Davidson, H.R.E. *Myths and Symbols in Pagan Europe.* Syracuse: University of Syracuse Press, 1988.

Delaney, Frank. *The Celts.* Boston: Little, Brown, 1986

Derolez, Rene. *Runica Manuscripta.* Brugge: Rijksuniversiteit te Gent, 1954.

De Vries, Jan. *Keltische Religion.* Stuttgart: Kohlhammer, 1961.

Graves, Robert. *The White Goddess.* New York: Farrar, Straus and Giroux, 1966, 2nd ed. [orig. published 1948]

Grieve, M. *A Modern Herbal.* New York: Dover, 1971 [orig. published 1931]

Lehmann, Ruth P. and Winfrid P. Lehmann. *An Introduction to Old Irish.* New York: The Modern Lanugage Association, 1975.

Littleton, C.S. *The New Comparative Mythology.* Berkeley: University of Califorinia Press, 1982.

Macalister, R. A. Stewart. *The Secret Languages of Ireland.* Cambridge: Cambridge University Press, 1937.

Macalister, R. A. Stewart. *Corpus inscriptionum insularum celticarum*. Dublin: Irish Manuscripts Commission, 1945.

MacCrossan, Tadhg. *The Sacred Cauldron: Secrets of the Druids*. St. Paul, MN: Llewellyn, 1991.

Matthews, Caitlin. *The Elements of the Celtic Tradition*. Longmead, UK: Element Books, 1989.

Matthews, John and Caitlin. *The Aquarian Guide to British and Irish Mythology*. Wellingborough, UK: Aquarian, 1988.

Murray, Liz and Colin. *The Celtic Tree Oracle*. London: Rider, 1988.

Pennick, Nigel. *Games of the Gods: The Origin of Board Games in Magic and Divination*. York Beach, ME: Weiser, 1989.

Piggott, Stuart *The Druids*. London: Thames and Hudson, 1968

Rees, Alwyn and Brinley. *Celtic Heritage: Ancient Tradition in Ireland and Wales*. London: Thames and Hudson, 1961.

Thorsson, Edred. *Runelore: A Handbook of Esoteric Runology*. York Beach, ME: Weiser, 1987.

Tolstoy, Nikolai. *The Quest for Merlin*. Boston: Little, Brown, 1985.

STAY IN TOUCH

On the following pages you will find listed, with their current prices, some of the books now available on related subjects. Your book dealer stocks most of these and will stock new titles in the Llewellyn series as they become available. We urge your patronage.

To obtain our full catalog, to keep informed about new titles as they are released and to benefit from informative articles and helpful news, you are invited to write for our bimonthly news magazine/catalog, *Llewellyn's New Worlds of Mind and Spirit*. A sample copy is free, and it will continue coming to you at no cost as long as you are an active mail customer. Or you may subscribe for just $10.00 in the U.S.A. and Canada ($20.00 overseas, first class mail). Many book-stores also have *New Worlds* available to their customers. Ask for it.

Stay in touch! In *New Worlds'* pages you will find news and features about new books, tapes and services, announcements of meetings and seminars, articles helpful to our readers, news of authors, products and services, special money-making opportunities, and much more.

Llewellyn's New Worlds of Mind and Spirit
P.O. Box 64383-783, St. Paul, MN 55164-0383, U.S.A.
* * *

TO ORDER BOOKS AND TAPES

If your book dealer does not have the books described on the following pages readily available, you may order them directly from the publisher by sending full price in U.S. funds, plus $3.00 for postage and handling for orders *under* $10.00; $4.00 for orders *over* $10.00. There are no postage and handling charges for orders over $50.00. Postage and handling rates are subject to change. UPS Delivery: We ship UPS whenever possible. Delivery guaranteed. Provide your street address as UPS does not deliver to P.O. Boxes. Allow 4-6 weeks for delivery. UPS to Canada requires a $50.00 minimum order. Orders outside the U.S.A. and Canada: Air-mail—add retail price of book; add $5.00 for each non-book item (tapes, etc.); add $1.00 per item for surface mail.

FOR GROUP STUDY AND PURCHASE

Because there is a great deal of interest in group discussion and study of the sub-ject matter of this book, we feel that we should encourage the adoption and use of this particular book by such groups by offering a special quantity price to group leaders or agents.

Our special quantity price for a minimum order of five copies of *The Book of Ogham* is $38.85 cash-with-order. This price includes postage and handling within the United States. Minnesota residents must add 6.5% sales tax. For additional quantities, please order in multiples of five. For Canadian and foreign orders, add postage and handling charges as above. Credit card (VISA, MasterCard, Ameri-can Express) orders are accepted. Charge card orders only ($15.00 minimum order) may be phoned in free within the U.S.A. or Canada by dialing 1-800-THE-MOON. For customer service, call 1-612-291-1970. Mail orders to:

LLEWELLYN PUBLICATIONS
P.O. Box 64383-783, St. Paul, MN 55164-0383, U.S.A.

Prices subject to change without notice.

NORTHERN MAGIC
Mysteries of the Norse, Germans & English
by Edred Thorsson

This in-depth primer of the magic of the Northern Way introduces the major concepts and practices of Gothic or Germanic magic. English, German, Dutch, Icelandic, Danish, Norwegian, and Swedish peoples are all directly descended from this ancient Germanic cultural stock. According to author Edred Thorsson, if you are interested in living a holistic life with unity of body-mind-spirit, a key to knowing your spiritual heritage is found in the heritage of your body—in the natural features which you have inherited from your distant ancestors. Most readers of this book already "speak the language" of the Teutonic tradition.

Northern Magic contains material that has never before been discussed in a practical way. This book outlines the ways of Northern magic and the character of the Northern magician. It explores the theories of traditional Northern psychology (or the lore of the soul) in some depth, as well as the religious tradition of the Troth and the whole Germanic theology. The remaining chapters make up a series of "mini-grimoires" on four basic magical techniques in the Northern Way: Younger Futhark rune magic, Icelandic galdor staves, Pennsylvania hex signs, and "seith" (or shamanism). This is an excellent overview of the Teutonic tradition that will interest neophytes as well as long-time travelers along the Northern Way.

0-87542-782-0, 224 pgs., mass market, illus.   **$4.95**

A BOOK OF TROTH
by Edred Thorsson

One of the most widespread of the ancient pagan revivals is Asatru or Odinism. Its followers seek to rekindle the way of the North, of the ancient Teutonic peoples. Until now, no book has completely expressed the nature and essence of that movement *A Book of Troth* is that book.

This is the most traditional and well-informed general guide to the practice of the elder Germanic folk way. An official document of the organization known as the "Ring of Troth," *A Book of Troth* is not a holy book or bible in the usual sense. Rather, it outlines a code of behavior and a set of actions, not a doctrine or a way of believing.

A Book of Troth presents for the first time the essence of Teutonic heathenry between two covers. It is a must for anyone interested in an effective system based on ancient and timeless principles.

0-87542-777-4, 244 pgs., 5.25 x 8, illus.   **$9.95**

RUNE MIGHT
Secret Practices of the German Rune Magicians
by Edred Thorsson
Rune Might reveals, for the first time in the English language, the long-hidden secrets of the German rune magicians who practiced their arts in the beginning of the century. By studying the contents of *Rune Might* and working with the exercises, the reader will be introduced to a fascinating world of personalities and the sometimes sinister dark corners of runic history. Beyond this, the reader will be able to experience the direct power of the runes as experienced by the early German rune magicians.

Rune Might takes the best and most powerful of the runic techniques developed in that early phase of the runic revival and offers them as a coherent set of exercises. Experience rune yoga, rune-dance, runic hand gestures (mudras), rune singing (mantras), group rites with runes, runic healing, runic geomancy, and two of the most powerful runic methods of engaging transpersonal powers: the Ritual of the Ninth Night and the Ritual of the Grail Cup.

The exercises represent bold new methods of drawing magical power into your life—regardless of the magical tradition or system with which you normally work. No other system does this in quite the direct and clearly defined ways that rune exercises do.
0-87542-778-2, 176 pgs., 5.25 x 8, illus.   **$7.95**

THE NINE DOORS OF MIDGARD:
A Complete Curriculum of Rune Magic
by Edred Thorsson
The Nine Doors of Midgard are the gateways to self-transformation through the runes. This is the complete course of study and practice which has successfully been in use inside the Rune-Gild for ten years. Now it is being made available to the public for the first time.

The runic tradition represents a whole school of magic with the potential of becoming the equal of the Hermetic or Cabalistic tradition. The runic tradition is the northern or Teutonic equivalent of the Hermetic tradition of the south. *The Nine Doors of Midgard* is the only manual to take a systematic approach to initiation into runic practices.

Through nine lessons or stages in a graded curriculum, the books takes the rune student from a stage in which no previous knowledge of runes or esoteric work is assumed to a fairly advanced stage of initiation. The book also contains a complete reading course in outside material.
0-87542-781-2, 320 pgs., 5.25 x 8, illus.   **$12.95**

THE SACRED CAULDRON
Secrets of the Druids
by Tadhg MacCrossan

Here is a comprehensive course in the history and development of Celtic religious lore, the secrets taught by the Druids, and a guide to the modern performance of the rites and ceremonies as practiced by members of the "Druidactos," a spiritual organization devoted to the revival of this ancient way of life.

The Sacred Cauldron evolved out of MacCrossan's extensive research in comparative mythology and Indo-European linguistics, etymology and archaeology. He has gone beyond the stereotypical image of standing stones and white-robed priests to piece together the truth about Druidism.The reader will find detailed interpretations of the words, phrases and titles that are indigenous to this ancient religion. Here also are step-by-step instructions for ceremonial rites for modern-day practice.

0-87542-103-2, 302 pgs., 5.25 x 8, illus. $10.95

CELTIC MAGIC
by D. J. Conway

Many people, not all of Irish descent, have a great interest in the ancient Celts and the Celtic pantheon, and *Celtic Magic* is the map they need for exploring this ancient and fascinating magical culture.

Celtic Magic is for the reader who is either a beginner or intermediate in the field of magic. It provides an extensive "how-to" of practical spellworking. There are many books on the market dealing with the Celts and their beliefs, but none guide the reader to a practical application of magical knowledge for use in everyday life. There is also an in-depth discussion of Celtic deities and the Celtic way of life and worship, so that an intermediate practitioner can expand upon the spellwork to build a series of magical rituals. Presented in an easy-to-understand format, *Celtic Magic* is for anyone searching for new spells that can be worked immediately, without elaborate or rare materials, and with minimal time and preparation.

0-87542-136-9, 240 pgs., mass market, illus. $3.95

RUNE MAGIC
by Donald Tyson
Drawing upon historical records, poetic fragments, and the informed study of scholars, *Rune Magic* resurrects the ancient techniques of this tactile form of magic and integrates those methods with modern occultism so that anyone can use the runes in a personal magical system. For the first time, every known and conjectured meaning of all 33 known runes, including the 24 runes known as "futhark", is available in one volume. In addition, *Rune Magic* covers the use of runes in divination, astral traveling, skrying, and on amulets and talismans. A complete rune ritual is also provided, and 24 rune words are outlined. Gods and Goddesses of the runes are discussed, with illustrations from the National Museum of Sweden.
0-87542-826-6, 224 pgs., 6 x 9, photos   **$9.95**

RUNE MAGIC CARDS
by Donald Tyson
Llewellyn Publications presents, for the first time ever, Rune Magic Cards created by Donald Tyson. This unique divinatory deck consists of 24 strikingly designed cards, boldly portraying a Germanic "futhark" Rune on each card. Robin Wood has illuminated each Rune Card with graphic illustrations done in the ancient Norse tradition. Included on each card are the old English name, its meaning, the phonetic value of the Rune, and its number in Roman numerals. Included with this deck is a complete instruction booklet, giving the history and origins, ways of using the cards for divination, and magical workings, sample spreads and a wealth of information culled from years of study.
0-87542-827-4, boxed set: 24 two-color cards, 48-pg. booklet   **$12.95**

LEAVES OF YGGDRASIL
Runes, Gods, Magic, Feminine Mysteries, Folklore
by Freya Aswynn

Leaves of Yggdrasil is the first book to offer an extensive presentation of Rune concepts, mythology and magical applications inspired by Dutch/Frisian traditional lore.

Author Freya Aswynn, although writing from a historical perspective, offers her own interpretations of this data based on her personal experience with the system. Freya's inborn, native gift of psychism enables her to work as a runic seer and consultant in psychological rune readings, one of which is detailed in a chapter on "Runic Divination."

Leaves of Yggdrasil emphasizes the feminine mysteries and the function of the Northern priestesses. It unveils a complete and personal system of the rune magic that will fascinate students of mythology, spirituality, psychism and Teutonic history, for this is not only a religious autobiography but also a historical account of the ancient Northern European culture.

0-87542-024-9, 288 pgs., 5.25 x 8   **$12.95**

A PRACTICAL GUIDE TO THE RUNES
Their Uses in Divination and Magick
by Lisa Peschel

At last the world has a beginners book on the Nordic runes that is written in straightforward and clear language. Each of the 25 runes is elucidated through no-nonsense descriptions and clean graphics. A rune's altered meaning in relation to other runes and its reversed position is also included. The construction of runes and accessories covers such factors as the type of wood to be used, the size of the runes, and the coloration, carving and charging of the runes. With this book the runes can be used in magick to effect desired results. Talismans carved with runescripts or bindrunes allow you to carry your magick in a tangible form, providing foci for your will. Four rune layouts complete with diagrams are presented with examples of specific questions to ask when consulting the runes. Rather than simple fortunetelling devices, the runes are oracular, empowered with the forces of Nature. They present information for you to make choices in your life.

0-87542-593-3, 192 pgs., mass market, illus.   **$3.95**

SCOTTISH WITCHCRAFT
The History & Magick of the Picts
by Raymond Buckland

From the ancient misty Highlands of Scotland to modern-day America come the secrets of solitary Witchcraft practice. *Scottish Witchcraft* explores "PectiWita," or the craft of the Picts, the mysterious early Keltic people. The Scottish PectiWita tradition differs in many ways from the Wicca of England—there is little emphasis on the worship of the gods (though it is there), but more on the living and blending of magick into everyday life.

Many people attracted to modern-day Wicca are unable to contact or join a coven. PectiWita is a path for the solitary Witch; and here, for the first time, are full details of this solitary branch of the Old Ways. Learn the history of the Picts, their origins and beliefs. Learn how to make simple tools and use them to work magic. Through step-by-step instructions you are brought into touch and then into complete harmony with all of nature. Explore their celebrations, talismans, song and dance, herbal lore, runes and glyphs, and recipes. Learn how to practice the religion in the city and with groups.

0-87542-057-5, 256 pgs., 5.25 x 8, illus., photos $9.95

CIRCLES, GROVES & SANCTUARIES
Sacred Spaces of Today's Pagans
Compiled by Dan & Pauline Campanelli

Pagans and Wiccans have always been secretive people. Even many within the Craft have not been allowed to enter the sacred space of others. But within the pages of *Circles, Groves & Sanctuaries,* you are given the unique opportunity to examine, in intimate detail, the magical places created by Pagans and Witches across the country, around the world and from a wide variety of traditions.

Take guided tours of sacred spaces by the people who created them, and listen as they tell of the secret meanings and magical symbolism of the sometimes strange and always wonderful objects that adorn these places. Learn of their rituals that can be adapted by the most seasoned practitioner or the newest seeker on the hidden path. Become inspired to create your own magical space—indoors or out, large or small.

0-87542-108-3, 256 pgs., 7 x 10, 120 photos $12.95

THE FAMILY WICCA BOOK
The Craft for Parents & Children
by Ashleen O'Gaea

Enjoy the first book written for pagan parents! The number of Witches raising children to the Craft is growing. The need for mutual support is rising—yet until now, there have been no books that speak to a Wiccan family's needs and experience. Finally, here is *The Family Wicca Book*, full to the brim with rituals, projects, encouragement and practical discussion of real-life challenges. You'll find lots of ideas to use right away.

Is magic safe for children? Why do some people think Wiccans are Satanists? How do you make friends with spirits and little people in the local woods? Find out how one Wiccan family gives clear and honest answers to questions that intrigue pagans all over the world.

When you want to ground your family in Wicca without ugly "bashing;" explain life, sex and death without embarrassment; and add to your Sabbats without much trouble or expense, *The Family Wicca Book* is required reading. You'll refer to it again and again as your traditions grow with your family.

0-87542-591-7, 240 pgs., 5.25 x 8, illus., glossary, bibliography $9.95

BUCKLAND'S COMPLETE BOOK OF WITCHCRAFT
by Raymond Buckland

Here is the most complete resource to the study and practice of modern, non-denominational Wicca. This is a lavishly illustrated, self-study course for the solitary or group. Included are rituals; exercises for developing psychic talents; information on all major "sects" of the Craft; sections on tools, beliefs, dreams, meditations, divination, herbal lore, healing, ritual clothing and much, much more. This book unites theory and practice into a comprehensive course designed to help you develop into a practicing Witch, one of the "Wise Ones." It is written by Ray Buckland, a very famous and respected authority on Witchcraft who first came public with the Old Religion in the United States. Large format with workbook-type exercises, profusely illustrated and full of music and chants. Takes you from A to Z in the study of Witchcraft.

Never before has so much information on the Craft of the Wise been collected in one place. Traditionally, there are three degrees of advancement in most Wiccan traditions. When you have completed studying this book, you will be the equivalent of a Third-Degree Witch. Even those who have practiced Wicca for years find useful information in this book, and many covens are using this for their textbook. If you want to become a Witch, or if you merely want to find out what Witchcraft is really about, you will find no better book than this.

0-87542-050-8, 272 pgs., 8 1/2 x 11, illus. $14.95

BY STANDING STONE & ELDER TREE
Ritual and the Unconscious
by William Gray
Originally published in 1975 as *The Rollright Ritual*, this book is the re-release of this fascinating work complete with illustrations and a new introduction by the author. The famous stone circle of the "Rollrights" in Oxfordshire, England, is well known to folklorists. Gray, through the use of psychometry, has retrieved the story of the rocks from the rocks themselves, the story of the culture that placed them and the ritual system used by the ancient stone setters.

This book shows how you can create a Rollright Circle anywhere you wish, even in your own backyard, or within your own mind during meditation. Gray provides specific instructions and a script with an explanation of the language. Even for those not interested in performing the ritual, *By Standing Stone & Elder Tree* provides an exciting exploration of ancient cultures and of the value that stones hold for the fate of modern civilization.
0-87542-299-3, 208 pages, 5.25 x 8, illus.   **$9.95**

MAGICAL RITES FROM THE CRYSTAL WELL
by Ed Fitch
In nature, and in the earth, we look and find beauty. Within ourselves we find a well from which we may draw truth and knowledge. And when we draw from this well, we rediscover that we are all children of the Earth.

The simple rites in this book are presented to you as a means of finding your own way back to nature; for discovering and experiencing the beauty and the magic of unity with the source. These are the celebrations of the seasons; at the same time they are rites by which we attune ourselves to the flow of the force: the energy of life.

These are rites of passage by which we celebrate the major transitions we all experience in life. Here are the Old Ways, but they are also the Ways for Today.
0-87542-230-6, 160 pgs., 7 x 10, illus.   **$9.95**

WITCHCRAFT TODAY, BOOK ONE
The Modern Craft Movement
edited by Chas S. Clifton

For those already in the Craft, and for those who stand outside the ritual circle wondering if it is the place for them, *Witchcraft Today 1* brings together the writings of nine well-known Neopagans who give a cross-section of the beliefs and practices of this diverse and fascinating religion.

The contributors live in cities, small towns and rural areas, from California to Ireland, and they have all claimed a magical birthright—that lies open to any committed person—of healing, divination, counseling and working with the world's cycles.

Written specifically for this volume, the articles include:

- "A Quick History of Witchcraft's Revival" by Chas S. Clifton
- "An Insider's Look at Pagan Festivals" by Oz
- "Seasonal Rites and Magical Rites" by Pauline Campanelli
- "Witchcraft and Healing" by Morwyn
- "Sex Magic" by Valerie Voigt
- "Men and Women in Witchcraft" by Janet and Stewart Farrar
- "Witches and the Earth" by Chas S. Clifton
- "The Solo Witch" by Heather O'Dell
- "Witchcraft and the Law" by Pete Pathfinder Davis
- "Witchcraft and Shamanism" by Grey Cat
- "Being a Pagan in a 9-to-5 World" by Valerie Voigt

Also included are additional resources for Wiccans including publications, mail order suppliers, pagan organizations, computer bulletin boards and special-interest resources. The Principles of Wiccan Belief are also restated here.

0-87542-377-9, 208 pgs., 5.25 x 8   **$9.95**

WHEEL OF THE YEAR
Living the Magical Life
by Pauline Campanelli, illus. by Dan Campanelli
If you feel elated by the celebrations of the Sabbats and hunger for that feeling during the long weeks between Sabbats, *Wheel of the Year* can help you put the joy and fulfillment of magic into your everyday life. This book shows you how to celebrate the lesser changes in Nature. The wealth of seasonal rituals and charms are all easily performed with materials readily available and are simple and concise enough that the practitioner can easily adapt them to work within the framework of his or her own Pagan tradition.

Learn to perform fire magic in November, the secret Pagan symbolism of Christmas tree ornaments, the best time to visit a fairy forest or sacred spring and what to do when you get there. Learn the charms and rituals and the making of magical tools that coincide with the nesting season of migratory birds. Whether you are a newcomer to the Craft or have found your way back many years ago, *Wheel of the Year* will be an invaluable reference book in your practical magic library. It is filled with magic and ritual for everyday life and will enhance any system of Pagan Ritual.
0-87542-091-5, 176 pgs., 7 x 10, illus.   **$9.95**

YEAR OF MOONS, SEASON OF TREES
Mysteries and Rites of Celtic Tree Magick
by Pattalee Glass-Koentop
Many of you are drawn to Wicca, or the Craft, but do not have teachers or like-minded people around to show you how the religion is practiced. *Year of Moons, Season of Trees* serves as that teacher and as a sourcebook. Most of Witchcraft in America comes from or has been influenced by that of the British Isles. The Druidic sacred trees native to that culture are the focus of this book. The essence, imagery and mythology behind the trees and seasons is vividly portrayed. Pattalee's explanations give subtle meanings that will be remembered long after the rite is complete.
0-87542-269-1, 264 pgs., 7 x 10, illus.   **$14.95**

Prices subject to change without notice.

THE 21 LESSONS OF MERLYN
A Study in Druid Magic & Lore
by Douglas Monroe

For those with an inner drive to touch genuine Druidism—or who feel that the lore of King Arthur touches them personally—*The 21 Lessons of Merlyn* will come as an engrossing adventure and psychological journey into history and magic. This is a complete introductory course in Celtic Druidism, packaged within the framework of 21 authentic and expanded folk story/ lessons that read like a novel. These lessons, set in late Celtic Britain ca A.D. 500, depict the training and initiation of the real King Arthur at the hands of the real Merlyn-the-Druid: one of the last great champions of Paganism within the dawning age of Christianity. As you follow the boy Arthur's apprenticeship from his first encounter with Merlyn in the woods, you can study your own program of Druid apprenticeship with the detailed practical ritual applications that follow each story. The 21 folk tales were collected by the author in Britain and Wales during a ten-year period; the Druidic teachings are based on the actual, never-before-published 16th-century manuscript entitled *The Book of Pheryllt*.
0-87542-496-1, 420 pgs., 6 x 9, illus., photos, softcover **$12.95**

THE TRUTH ABOUT THE DRUIDS
by Tadhg MacCrossan

To mention the word Druid is to evoke images of ancient wizards and wonder-workers from old Irish sagas or Welsh legends. The Druids have been credited as engineers of Stonehenge, as the priests of the Lost Tribes of ancient Israel, and as shamans of pre-Celtic Western Europe. They have been credited with Pythagorean philosophy, Cabala, mysteries of the Goddess, Buddhism, Runes and Wicca.

But these popular characterizations are not accurate representations of factual history. Just who, then, were the Druids?

The Truth About the Druids explores the oral tradition and the Druidic class, Celtic origins, Celtic religion and mythology, Druidic festivals and clothing, Celtic magic, Neo-druidism since the 1700s, and the future of Druidism

Druidism is the spiritual path that is in harmony with the natural flow of the cosmos. It is one of the many folk religions that brings people back into reverence for living things. Travel back to an ancient time in old Ireland before Patrick came to spread the religion of the Latin language, and discover *The Truth About the Druids*.
0-87542-577-1, 32 pgs., 5-1/2 x 8-1/2 **$2.00**